# THE ART OF CHICAGO IMPROV

## Short Cuts to Long-Form Improvisation

Rob Kozlowski

HEINEMANN ■ Portsmouth, NH

For my late mother

**Heinemann**
361 Hanover Street
Portsmouth, NH 03801–3912
www.heinemanndrama.com

*Offices and agents throughout the world*

**Library of Congress Cataloging-in-Publication Data**
Kozlowski, Rob.
The art of Chicago improv : short cuts to long-form improvisation /
Rob Kozlowski.
p. cm.
Includes bibliographical references.
ISBN 0-325-00384-X
1. Improvisation (Acting).    2. Comedy.
3. Stand-up comedy—Illinois—Chicago—History.
I. Title
PN2071 .I5 K69 2002
792'.028—dc21        2001051789

*Editor: Lisa A. Barnett*
*Production: Elizabeth Valway*
*Cover design: Jenny Jensen Greenleaf*
*Typesetter: Technologies    Typography, Inc.*
*Manufacturing: Steve Bernier*

T    &    C    D i g i t a l

# Contents

# **A**cknowledgments

'd like to extend a special thanks to all the people without whom there would be no book. The guilty parties include Liz Allen, Jack Bronis, Craig Cackowski, Rob Chambers, Chris Day, Doug Diefenbach, Kevin Dorff, Andy Eninger, Larrance Fingerhut, Mark Gagne, Susan Gaspar, Noah Gregoropoulos, Don Hall, Charna Halpern, Mark Henderson, Jim Jarvis, Cholley Kuhaneck, Kelly Leonard, Rob Mello, Kevin Mullaney, Mick Napier, Edmund O'Brien, Jonathan Pitts, Jackie Rosepal, Steve Scholz, David Shepherd, Brian Stack, Mark Sutton, and Nancy Howland Walker. Thank you to my wonderful fiancée, Aileen, for her boundless patience and assistance, my mother and father, my brother, Lisa Barnett, and all the teachers, directors, coaches, and performers that have inspired me in my pursuits. You know who you are.

# What Is Chicago Improv Anyway?

M y first experience with improv was in 1993 in a small apartment above a now-defunct bakery in Chicago's Old Town neighborhood, about a block south of the legendary Second City

> We were absolutely fearless about going on to do the world's most abysmal bullshit.
> —Del Close

Theatre. It was a night that changed my life, much the same way that improv has changed the lives of many people it has touched— performers and nonperformers alike. Unique among theatre disciplines in existing more as a philosophy of how to live rather than a philosophy of how to act on stage, improvisational acting can transform a shy schoolboy into a comedy legend.

When people talk about improv, they're talking about anything but stand-up comedy. As well as comics like Robin Williams and Jonathan Winters can improvise alone on a stage, they're not dealing with an ensemble of six or seven performers, each with fantastic imaginations and instincts. In stand-up there is no group agreement. You get to say whatever you want to say. There are those that believe stand-up is "funnier" than group improvisation, but there has never been a rule that improvisation *must* be funny. When the Second City was founded, it began a tradition of high comedy from improvisation and generations have continued that tradition. Whenever a production of serious improvisational theatre is attempted, often critics—unfamiliar with what improvisation really represents—will chide the show for not "being funny enough."

In *Truth in Comedy* (Close, Halpern, and Johnson 1994), ImprovOlympic cofounder Charna Halpern states, "One of the biggest mistakes an improviser can make is attempting to be funny" (23). The simple act of communicating with another person in everyday life is not filled with punch lines and wisecracks, unless you live inside a television sitcom. The humor that comes from improvisation grows organically, through the simple act of complete agreement.

Two words best describe the underlying philosophy of improvisation: "Yes and." "Yes and" is something so central to improvisation that ImprovOlympic named its production company Yes And Productions. Teachers around Chicago tell students to follow "yes and." It's pretty simple stuff. Take what your partner says, accept it, and build on it. Other rules soon followed. "Don't deny the established reality of a scene!" If my scene partner imagines she's holding an iguana and states it, then she's holding an iguana.

In one three-hour class, a person off the street can learn and memorize the few rules of improvisation that exist and then spend years untraining his ego to actually apply the rules to performance. There are few people on the earth who are ever raised to accept everything everyone says and then build on it. Those who do have probably had the stuffing beaten out of them at one time or another for being so agreeable. We live in a society of denial and argument.

In this environment, adults are taught to suppress their real feelings. A proclamation of love from a classmate will likely be rebuked. Often, the amorous person will be too fearful to make any such proclamation and the recipient of the love won't even have the chance to rebuke it. I learned that first night in class that in improvisation if love is proclaimed, the love must be accepted. "And I love *you!*" we were encouraged to say.

The first six words of Chapter 1 in Viola Spolin's masterwork *Improvisation for the Theater* are: "Everyone can act. Everyone can improvise" (Spolin, Sills, and Sills 1999, 1). These six words lay the foundation for the decades of devoted students and performers in Chicago and around the world. Spolin, whose improv games designed for children essentially created improvisation as we see it today, and her son Paul Sills, who cofounded the Second City, made Chicago their home and from it was created a kind of society within a society. Almost a church of thought.

Spolin's theory was that experience consisted of three elements of involvement: intellectual, physical, and intuitive. Spolin believed the third element, intuitive, was far too neglected in the world of education, and her improv games were designed to tap into intuition. One can train or learn intellectually with a collection of knowledge, one can train and learn physically through exercises. The games trained intuitive thinking.

Spolin was born in Chicago in 1906 and trained first to be a settlement worker at Neva Boyd's Group Work School at Chicago's Hull House. Group leadership, recreation, and social group work influenced Spolin and in 1939, she found herself as the drama supervisor of the WPA (Works Progress Administration) Recreational Project. It was there she developed the games that would "unlock the individual's capacity for self-expression." Spolin explained, "The games came out of necessity. I didn't sit at home and dream them up. When I had a problem [directing], I made up a game. When another problem came up, I just made up a new game" (interview, *Los Angeles Times*, May 26, 1974).

In 1946, she founded the Young Actors Company in Hollywood to teach her games to children. This went on until 1955, when she came back to Chicago to direct the Playwright's Theatre Club, which her son Paul Sills cofounded with David Shepherd and Eugene Troobnick. In the early to mid-fifties, Sills applied his mother's teachings to performance art. It was the root of the Compass Players, the Second City, and everything else that has come into American improv for nearly half a century.

The list of writers, actors, and directors who have come from an improvisational background is staggering. When you walk into the Second City in Chicago and witness the list of names of people who have worked there, including Alan Arkin, Alan Alda, Ed Asner (and we're just in the As!), you truly realize what a mark improvisation has made in the world of film, television, and theatre. Second City alumni are everywhere. Turn on CBS on Monday nights, for example, and there's Peter Boyle on *Everybody Loves Raymond*. Keep watching, and there's Jerry Stiller on *The King of Queens*.

What truly separates Second City from the improvisational theatres that have cropped up in the last twenty years is that Second City is based on the foundation that improvisation is a process to be used in the development of fully scripted comedy revues, rather than the product the audiences end up seeing on stage. (Most revues do feature an improvised sequence, and there is always a fully improvised, hour-long set following the scripted revue.)

A great divide in improvisational thinking developed from the works of Del Close, who is the most influential figure in the work since Spolin and Sills. His opinion was that one could garner an evening's entertainment from improvisation exclusively. Those attempts first surfaced in the late 1960s, when the volatile Close was fired from Second City (on one of many occasions) and moved to San Francisco to begin work with a group called the Committee. It was here that Close and company first began work on a form that would be called the Harold. As stated in *Truth in Comedy*, "the group was searching for some way to unite all their games, scenes, and techniques into one format; they developed a way to intertwine scenes, games, monologues, songs and all manner of performing techniques" (Close, Halpern, and Johnson 1994, 7).

From this came Del Close's further experiments with what would be known later as part of a movement called "long-form improvisation" and finally his union with Charna Halpern in 1983 at ImprovOlympic, which caused a revolution in American comedy.

In this book, we will attempt to follow the path of improvisational theatre to where it stands today in its birthplace, Chicago, where the majority of improvisers practice something we call long-form improvisation. Thousands of students study at Second City, ImprovOlympic, and other training centers in Chicago, creating a subcommunity within the rich community of Chicago theatre, where it seems everyone goes to learn the art of acting before learning the harsh lessons of the *business* of acting in New York and Los Angeles.

We will also look at the ImprovOlympic, and how Del Close's genius spawned dozens of imitators, all seeking to create an evening of theatre made up completely on the spot. Other forms created at ImprovOlympic, including the Deconstruction and the Movie, build on the teachings of Harold, creating more complex and difficult paths to discovery for both the performers and the audience.

And in the years since Close and Halpern revolutionized improvisation, other directors and performers have come to the forefront, examining further the possibilities of improv as performance art.

Much of what Close and Halpern did was contribute to something known as long-form improvisation. Various approaches to improvised performance make up the world of long form and we'll examine several of these long forms in detail, such as Noah Gregoropolous' Close Quarters, of which the premise—an hour-long set taking place within a building within fifteen minutes with a cast of twelve—proves to be one of the most challenging and rewarding forms ever performed in Chicago. There are Robert Mello's long-form shows utilizing the methods of Sanford Meisner in improvised performance. There is Sybil, a single person performing multiple characters in a Harold-like form.

The genius of people like Spolin, Sills, and Close was to create ideas as platforms for entire theatrical philosophies and movements, to excite and challenge the minds and hearts of performers.

Chicago is a town of theatre. Without the financial might of Los Angeles and New York but with a rugged can-do spirit, hundreds of actors perform for free every week. Storefronts that used to function as bookstores are transformed into theatres. Ever since Steppenwolf Theater, the birthplace of Gary Sinise, Joan Allen, John Malkovich, and so many others, began in a basement in Highland Park in the late 1970s, actors in Chicago have tried to replicate its success, sometimes performing in venues far less regal than basements.

We will look at some of the improvisational theatres that have been built in the last twenty years, many of which owe their existence to ImprovOlympic, whose building into a legend we will also examine. ImprovOlympic (or IO, as it is now known) was founded in 1981 by Charna Halpern and David Shepherd, but it wasn't until Shepherd left and Del Close entered the scene in short time that IO became a revolutionary force in the movement.

On a worldwide scope, improvisation has been around as long as theatre. For brevity's sake, we will focus on the past fifty years in Chicago and the changes that have taken place in improvisational theatre, beginning with David Shepherd's utopian vision of the Compass, a workers theatre where literally *anyone* could jump up on stage at any point during a performance and join in the revelry. The ideal of completely improvised performance has been the Holy

Grail for improvisers—students, teachers, and performers—for decades. Many have attempted to reach that Holy Grail by practicing long-form improvisation. More than a few improvisers have their own opinions about just what long-form improvisation is, and we will look at their opinions and how their work has reached the stage. How can a group of people cooperate enough to have a completely improvised show that an audience will want to pay for?

If you're unfamiliar with the wonders of Chicago improv and are considering making the big leap, hopefully this book will function as a primer. For those who have already performed in Chicago for years, it may expose you to some of the work that has been done over the past twenty years—amazing performances of which you may not be aware.

In looking at improvisation in Chicago, a look at how the work originated is important. Improv did not just start out as a way to get laughs. It actually began at the same place as the atomic bomb.

# 2    A Short History

There are plenty of skeptics in the world who believe that history teaches you nothing. However, with any art form, it gives the artist a sense of perspective to know where his or her art form came from. Not only did the Chicago performers who originated improvisational theatre in the 1950s share a birthplace with the atomic bomb but they were wickedly intelligent young men and women who were voraciously seeking a political voice in uncertain times.

Why study the history of your art form? In a film history program at a college or a university, a filmmaker needs to watch the ancient crude films of Lumiere and George Meleis in order to achieve a deeper understanding of the social and cultural impact of the origins of the art. Placing themselves in the role of an audience who has *never* seen a moving picture before, students can understand the terror that must have struck an audience that witnessed a moving train approaching it in a small theatre in Paris in 1895.

Unfortunately, we can't go back to 1895 to see actors perform live theatre. Once an audience has viewed the play or the improvised performance, the moment is gone. Although in recent years, videotapes of stage productions have been made available, those often fail to capture the moment, the sensory experience of *being there.* They do not exist in a box where students can access them and understand their origins. Thus, theatre history has its roots in the oral and written traditions. Stories are the best way to capture a time and place.

Comic legends in the nineteenth century and the first half of the twentieth century first plied their trade in touring companies and Vaudeville. Comics like Charlie Chaplin and Stan Laurel practiced in British music halls. W. C. Fields began as a juggler in Vaudeville whose act eventually evolved into one of his comedy sketches. Comedy teams like George Burns and Gracie Allen, Abbott and Costello, and hundreds of others recycled Vaudeville bits for decades but only those who had mastered those bits were able to find fame and fortune.

By the '30s and '40s Vaudeville had disappeared and the main thrust of comedy fell to individual performances in radio and motion pictures. Comedy ensembles were not the norm and those that existed often consisted of family members like the Marx Brothers. Comedy revolved around a single personality in films and radio, the main stars of which all came from Vaudeville. However, by the 1950s these stars were getting older and there was no new "training ground" in which comics could learn.

In the early 1950s, the Compass, the world's first improvisational theatre, was not founded to produce movie and television stars but to create comedy based on theatrical and political beliefs. Before World War II, comedy was almost always situational and little political satire was practiced, save for the great humorist Will Rogers and others of his ilk. Political satire was almost always practiced to merely poke fun. Rare was the comic who was honestly angry at the social state of America or with politicians. The Compass helped American comedy achieve a sense of social importance.

And then from the ashes of the Compass came the Second City, and the comedy revolution began. Vaudeville was no more and improv was king. Just as you can point to Vaudeville as the origin point of many comic actors in the first half of the twentieth century, so can you point to improvisational theatre as the origin point for a large portion of the important comic actors in the second half of the century.

Improvisational theatre did not begin with Viola Spolin. It had been around for centuries. The art of using some form of improvisation as an actor's and playwright's tool has been around since the beginnings of theatre. The Commedia Dell'Arte is the most direct ancestor to modern improvisational comedy.

The first records of Commedia Dell'Arte appear to originate from Tuscany, Italy, around 1550. And *its* roots came from the masked comedies of ancient Rome, both from "the works of dramatists like Plautus, and in the folk tradition of the character acting troupes." The form combined scripted dialogue, mime, and improvised dialogue.

Four main characters formed the center of dell'arte, with a wealth of supporting characters around them. One was Pantalone, "who usually was presented as either an elderly nobleman or as a bankrupt." There was Dottore, a "middle-aged neighbor of Pantalone, either his friend or a bitter enemy. He is presented as a professional—a doctor or a lawyer or sometimes a charlatan" (*shift.merriweb.com.au/characters/commedia.html*). There was Harlequin, who was Pantalone's servant although he would often scoff at his duties. Harlequin represented the younger generation, the satirical voice of the troupe. Either Scapino or Brighella would be the fourth character, either one another servant of Pantalone. Brighella was a cunning and witty schemer around whom much of the plot or intrigue of the piece would be revolved. Scapino was somewhat like Brighella, but more of a bumbler and less of a schemer.

The characters would exist in one of several stock scenarios, inside of which they would improvise, drawing on the audience's familiarity with the characters to unify the various performances. Certain characteristics of Pantalone's would be repeated in performance after performance, and the audience's identification with that repetition would result in comic situations. This kind of humor, coming from the audience's identification with recurring characters, has been repeated countless times with television sitcom characters of today.

As Janet Coleman explains in her book *The Compass: The Improvisational Theatre That Revolutionized American Comedy,* the troupes who performed Commedia Dell'Arte were all-around entertainers. The Italian "improvisators" were all well versed in poetry, geography, foreign languages, history, and all manners of other subjects. They not only composed their own scenarios but also played musical instruments and sang. They were acrobatic. They were specialists in pantomime. As Coleman recounts, "While holding a glass of water, the great Vincentini would turn a somersault. Another Italian actor, famous for the way he played the sword-swinging bully Scaramouche, was reputedly so agile that he could box the ear of a fellow actor with his foot" (1990, 91).

The Commedia Dell'Arte eventually relied less on improvisation and evolved into more intricate, costumed entertainment until the late eighteenth century, when it evolved into Vaudeville and other forms of theatre.

The twentieth-century improvisers that would emerge in Chicago were at least as learned as their sixteenth-century counterparts (although few, if any, were as acrobatic). As described in Coleman's book, the roots of modern improvisational theatre were not only laid in the Commedia Dell'Arte and the classes of Viola Spolin but also in something called the "Chicago Experiment."

The Chicago Experiment was the brainchild of Chancellor Robert Maynard Hutchins, president of the University of Chicago from 1931 to 1951. He was inspired by the medieval university of Saint Thomas Aquinas. His strategy was to expose students to the "glories of contemplative life" (Coleman 1990, 3).

Hutchins hoped to create a body of intellectuals who would seek "enlightenment through a common body of ideas and information and by sharing the divine revelations of knowledge" (Coleman, 3). He threw away the age requirement for entrance into the University of Chicago and created fourteen exams, which, if one were able to complete satisfactorily, got you into school whether you were twelve or one hundred twelve. Thus, the University of Chicago became a haven for all sorts of intellectuals who couldn't hold a conversation without reciting a word from an obscure German playwright or two. They were the kind of people that you might hate for their brilliance and worldliness.

Into this atmosphere came the strange and the brilliant, many of whom one would not associate with the origin of Chicago improvisational theatre. There was, however, one name associated with the theatre that would indeed be the perfect person to help launch the embryonic stage of improv: Paul Sills. The son of Viola Spolin, he had already become a noted director at the University Theatre next to the University of Chicago's campus by 1952. At the time, the university lacked a school of drama and thus enterprising undergraduates needed to create one of their own. Hence, the creation of University Theatre. The actors involved were odd geniuses whose keen grasp of all things literary and intellectual made them marvels to watch. Severn Darden, for example, was one University Theatre performer who spent his undergraduate days wearing a cape.

At University Theatre, Sills would employ his mother's theatre games—including Who Am I?, Gibberish Teaching, Camera, Contact, and the Mirror Exercises—in rehearsals and workshops. The shows, however, were not improvisationally created. They were real, live plays written by playwrights both live and dead. For example, one season included *The Typewriter*, by Jean Cocteau, and *The Caucasian Chalk Circle*, by Berthold Brecht.

The latter show was particularly important in identifying both the aesthetic and political ideologies present in the early days of improvisational theatre. Coleman writes, "It seems obvious that even without sharing his political ideology, Sills would embrace Brecht's ideas for making the theatre reflective of real political conditions and accessible to people who might be interested in changing them" (1990, 36). Besides nurturing his evolving Marxist beliefs, Brecht's goal was to avoid the traditional wall between actor and audience. Rather than attempting to make the audience believe in the locations and characters, he wanted the audience to be completely aware that they were in a theatre, watching actors on a stage.

This ran completely contrary to the previous belief that you—as playwright, actor, and director—wish to take the audience members far away from the reality of the actual places in which they sit. No, here, the audience is participant, and those who have performed and watched improv over the years know it is often the very interactivity itself that lends much entertainment value to what occurs on stage.

Thus, Paul Sills, Mike Nichols, Severn Darden, Sheldon Patinkin, and many others were in the right place in the right time. The intellectual climate at the University of Chicago in the mid-'50s was vigorous; its political tenor, passionate. These were writers and performers that had something to say.

Then, the University Theatre evolved into the Playwrights Theatre Club, which marked the union of Paul Sills and David Shepherd.

David Shepherd knew nothing of Sills' mother, Viola Spolin, or her works in improvisation; his first exposure to her work was when she joined Playwrights as a director. Rather than coming from an improvisational background, Shepherd was a seemingly aimless drifter, a young man who had hitchhiked to Chicago with ten thousand dollars that he had inherited, obsessed with building a working-class theatre he wanted to call the Compass.

Shepherd had spent time in Europe studying cabaret theatre. His original hope was to build a cabaret theatre that would become a center of joy for some small Midwestern town, a small socialist utopia where anyone could get on stage at any time and improvise for his or her fellow man. No small Midwestern town seemed appropriate, so instead Shepherd headed to the biggest Midwestern town of them all.

Shepherd wrote in his journal: "I think that any theatre written for the working class will have to use simpler forms than those of the contemporary theatre, which is an expression of the middle class. I don't believe you can keep a working class audience awake during a play written in the style of Ibsen or Arthur Miller" (Coleman 1990, 47).

Shepherd, although plainly seeing that the Playwrights Theatre Club was far from his vision of the Compass as the "people's cabaret," still invested seven thousand dollars of his inherited money in the venture. Many improvisers today little realize that the world's first improvisational theatre had its roots in good, old-fashioned plays written by the world's greatest playwrights. Schnitzler's *Rounddance,* the sexual merry-go-round set in postwar Vienna that Max Ophuls had made into the film *LaRonde,* for example, was one of their opening season's productions. Plays like *The Dybbuk* and T. S. Eliot's *Murder in the Cathedral* were only a few of the works being presented on their stage in a Chicago that at the time was far from the vibrant center of theatre it is today. This kind of vibrant artistic commitment was a bit of a jolt to a town starved for live theatre and the ensemble only grew stronger upon adding other future Compass players like Elaine May.

Despite that artistic commitment, Shepherd, the chief investor, soon became disenchanted. In his journal, Shepherd wrote, "In a year and a half, I have helped build a miserable self-centered arts club which talks over the heads of its bourgeois members at the same time it licks their feet for patronage" (Coleman 1990, 78).

Shepherd's new contempt for the venture doomed it. The Playwrights Theatre Club soon folded. After its demise, Shepherd decided to resurrect his dream of a cabaret theatre called the Compass, believing that a script could stand up well in a rowdy environment as long as the pace was fast, the scenes were short, and the ensemble was limited to five or six actors each playing multiple roles. According to Shepherd's diaries, he tried to find new kinds of plays, "more efficient, theatrical, poetic and morally aware than the current product" (Coleman 1990, 83). His former collaborator Paul Sills was aboard, along with many other members of the Playwrights Theater Club, and all had the necessary theatrical acumen to perform those multiple roles in these plays.

There was one problem, however. Shepherd couldn't find the plays. Since the plays didn't exist yet, Shepherd and his company would have to create the plays themselves. Thus, the scenario play was born, a play with the beats of the story written in for the actors to improvise. Thanks to the scenario play, Shepherd and company were able to realize his dream of a cabaret theatre, and the Compass was born. Coleman (1990) calls the scenario play the first improvised "long form." Not only was improvisational theatre born but the idea of long-form improvisation as well.

Roger Bowen, who put together the first scenario play, *Enterprise,* outlined seven scenes and also used Stanislavsky's "internal action" technique. Stanislavsky was one of the great acting teachers of the twentieth century, and many of his methods were interpreted by American teachers to create the Method. Stanislavsky believed that actors needed to understand their characters' internal actions, such as "the goals, fears, ambitions, and wishes, from which all external actions spring." Bowen supplied characters in the scenario with internal actions. For example, one character in the scenario is "hypnotized by automobiles and having no other motive than getting a better car." Another regards "going to work as the greatest danger in life" (Coleman 1990, 87). He also gave the ensemble characteristics of group behavior.

Within this scenario, the actors would improvise and in the early days of the Compass, they showcased a new scenario play every week. However, it was not long before the cast felt the stress and strain of such a rigorous schedule, and then each individual play began to have longer runs. Then the scenarios slowly disappeared, replaced by shorter pieces. And not only was there improvisation in the performances but these shorter scenes would be perfected and performed on stage after improvising them over and over again. The roots of the Second City revue were evolving, although the scenario plays seen in the first days of the Compass were brought back once in a while.

Thanks to the difficulties in obtaining proper entertainment licenses and a general malaise in the finances of the operation, as well as problems with collecting enough actors for rehearsal, the Compass kept moving over and over again despite the artistic innovation and its growing popularity. Finally, after a relatively short amount of time, the Chicago Compass Players shut down their operations in the winter of 1956/1957.

It was, however, not the end of the Compass everywhere. In St. Louis, a Compass sprang up in 1957, directed by Theodore Flicker. He and Shepherd had also tried to open one up in New York but philosophical differences sprang up, a recurring theme in the career of David Shepherd.

In Sweet's book *Something Wonderful Right Away* (1978), Flicker reflected, "David was disgusted with my show. It was the first improvisational theater that had been a financial success, but he was horrified that I kept insisting that it be a show and that I put a time limit on improvisations, and that we'd do some things just for laughs" (160).

While the Compass ended, many of the performers who built it were far from defeated. When the always-passionate Paul Sills saw the huge success that former Compass colleagues Mike Nichols and Elaine May were becoming as a comedy team, he was inspired. Sills in 1959 was working at a nightclub called the Gate of Horn. His experiences there contributed to his belief that a club featuring improvisational theatre could be successful. Joining him in his new venture as co-owners were Bernie Sahlins and Howard Alk. The first cast featured a number of former Compass players—Alk, Roger Bowen, Severn Darden, Andrew Duncan, Barbara Troobnick—and a newcomer named Mina Kolb. The new venture would be called the Second City.

Second City did not employ scenario plays at all. Rather, like they would continue to do for over four decades, they used improvisation as part of the rehearsal process to write scenes as part of revues, which were often titled with puns and plays on words like

*Economy of Errors* or *Slaughterhouse 5, Cattle 0.* Some revues in the early days featured scenes that would span an entire act, a practice that eventually faded. After the revue, the company would improvise a practice set, which would be open to the general public for free.

On December 16, 1959, the Second City opened its doors at 1842 North Wells Street, in what used to be a Chinese laundry. It became an immediate smash hit, becoming the sort of sensation in the matter of a few months that most theatres never achieve. The timing was right for this kind of cabaret theatre, where audience members could sip cocktails at their seats while the performers spouted out wicked political and social satire, wearing snappy suits and cocktail dresses on stage.

The late '50s and early '60s were the age of the beginning of hard-edged satire. It was the age of Lenny Bruce. Audiences were now sophisticated enough to poke fun at themselves and their rulers. Comedians like Bruce started getting thrown in jail for saying things that today's comedians would consider tame. Second City came along at exactly the right time.

Very quickly, the Second City went national. In July 1961 the first company had a very successful run at the Ivar Theater in Los Angeles. The first of very few failures in their history, a Broadway engagement called *From the Second City* was a commercial disappointment, but in January 1962 they began a new run in a Greenwich Village nightclub called the Square East. They were there for four and a half years.

Two of the New York directors, Alan Myerson and Larry Arrick, had philosophical differences with Sills. Myerson left to form the Committee in San Francisco, which ran from April 1963 till October 1973. The Committee, with Myerson and fellow Second City refugee Del Close, became the birthplace of the long-form Harold. Another Second City alumnus, Theodore J. Flicker, started the Premise, which ran from November 1960 until 1963/1964. Both the Premise and the Committee were highly successful projects, the first of many that would come from the minds of Second City alumni.

Very soon the Second City opened a second theatre in Chicago, Playwrights at Second City. Playwrights opened at 1846 North Wells, but the two theatres soon switched spaces (Playwrights had the larger one). The venture was simply an attempt by Second City members to retain some of their theatrical backgrounds in presenting previously written plays. Playwrights, however, ended soon afterward.

In the early 1960s Paul Sills left Second City. He then turned to experimentation with his mother, Viola. In 1965, they started Game Theater, in which members from the audience would go up on stage and play the Spolin games. In 1969, Sills began the Body Politic, another experiment in what he called "Story Theater," in which characters narrate their own actions on the stage. Loftier than the populist Second City, their first show was Ovid's *Metamorphoses: Love Lives of the Gods.*

Over the years, Sills has continued to work on Story Theater and now lives semi-retired in Wisconsin, spending summers teaching the games that he and his mother made famous. He even released a third edition of *Improvisation for the Theater* several years after his mother died, with new games that captured the spirit of the original games that Spolin had made the foundation of improvisation.

The theatre that Paul Sills had helped to build, meanwhile, quickly became legendary. When one walks into the Second City in Chicago, the list of names is a who's who of comic celebrities. Some of the personalities who graced the stages of Second City in the 1960s were Joan Rivers, Robert Klein, Avery Schreiber, Paul Sand, Del Close, David Steinberg, Fred Willard, and dozens more.

However, it was the 1970s that truly made the Second City a household name around the country. A couple of events occurred that would catapult Second City from the status of "successful theatre" to "legend." First and foremost was the opening of the Second City Toronto in 1973, which introduced Dan Akyroyd, John Candy, Gilda Radner, Eugene Levy, and others to the world. The Toronto company put together a television show under the auspices of Andrew Alexander, owner of Second City Toronto, the premise of which was an imaginary television station called SCTV. And, of course, there was *Saturday Night Live,* the original cast of which featured numerous Second City cast members from both the Chicago and Toronto stages.

The source of the success of these shows was not lost on the general public. Soon, the Second City was legendary. Actors and writers from the theatre had already become successful but the pop revolution that resulted from the two television shows made the theatre world famous. The lure of that fame would bring many actors to Chicago to try to make it at Second City so they could be seen and cast in *Saturday Night Live.*

While gaining an international reputation, the Second City continued to run the successful resident companies in Chicago and Toronto, each of which operated its own touring companies that would feature old scenes and would function as a training ground for potential resident players. On the Chicago Mainstage, veteran Del Close directed the vast majority of shows, and he was mentor to many of the performers who would later gain fame in film and television.

In 1982, the Second City helped open a space for Paul Sills to have workshops and Story Theater shows. The space was right behind the Chicago Mainstage in the Piper's Alley complex. Once Sills left, they turned it into a cabaret space for the Practical Theater company, a comedy troupe of Northwestern grads including Julia Louis-Dreyfus, Brad Hall, and Gary Kroger. That company soon folded because *Saturday Night Live* hired much of the cast and the immediate gutting of talent forced the troupe out of business.

Then, Second City took it over, using the space to present old material with the Touring Company. Director Don DePollo and the cast, however, were itching to add their own material, something that touring companies weren't supposed to be allowed to do. It wasn't until owner Bernie Sahlins was out of town that Don DePollo and his cast covertly wrote a whole new revue, called it *Cows on Ice,* and opened it to rave reviews. The Second City e.t.c. was born.

Sahlins sold the Second City in 1985 to Andrew Alexander and Len Stuart, who already owned the Toronto theatre. He continued directing until 1988, when he said, "I realized I had no one left to talk to. The new generations were all weaned on television. That was their frame of reference. The original group had come out of the University of Chicago, then the Beat Generation, even the so-called 'Next Generation' were a group that came from a theatrical and literary base. They were children of the television age, sure, but they were intellectual about it."

In the late 1980s, with the departure of Sahlins, the Second City was in a minor crisis. Sure, it was making plenty of money and there looked to be no end to the theatre in a climate in which theatres seemed to open and close on a daily basis. Alexander was the consummate businessman and knew how to run his theatre.

However, as the thirtieth anniversary of the Second City approached, bags under the theatre's eyes began to appear. Critics were bored. As described in Patinkin's book *The Second City* (2000, 155) Tony Adler revealed that "the typical *Reader* review of any current Second City show starts out talking about the great old shows of legend—the ones nobody actually could have seen, where Mike Nichols and Gilda Radner did patient/therapist routines while Severn Darden and John Belushi ran drills for the U of C football team. The review then explains why the current show is a complete pathetic betrayal of everything those old shows stood for."

After Bernie Sahlins left the director's chair, Alexander was in the unenviable position of auditioning new directors. For the past twenty years it had almost been exclusively Bernie Sahlins or Del Close directing the company, so Alexander turned to Del Close, who had spent the last seven years revolutionizing improv at ImprovOlympic (about which we'll read more in the next chapter). Close proceeded to fire most of the previous cast and brought on a new cast consisting of ImprovOlympic performers, including Chris Farley and Tim Meadows (who later were the first Second City people cast on *SNL* in quite some time, justifying again Close's unerring eye for talent). However, the revue was a disaster.

It was, according to Sheldon Patinkin in *The Second City* book, "dark, often misogynistic, and occasionally confusing to many of our audiences" (2000, 161). Many critics felt the revue seemed unfinished and actually was. Seemingly losing interest in the process of rehearsing, two weeks before the show was due to open, Close announced that the show was ready and halted the process.

Patinkin recalls, "But the show was a harbinger of things to come. It had an edge that many who'd been criticizing us felt had been missing for too long. For them, the 'formula' at least wasn't as apparent as it had been recently. Furthermore, part of what was occasionally confusing to our more traditional and formerly content audiences was that not everything was as neatly plotted out as they were expecting; the scenes weren't always the traditional beginning-middle-end ones they were used to. Along with his personal worldview, Del had also brought a little of the more

fragmented structure of his long-form improvisation to the show"
(2000, 161).

But probably the most important development for the Second
City was the development of a formal training center during the late
1980s. Don DePollo and other Second City directors had been running fairly informal workshops for years but Alexander decided to
do away with the informality and begin a strict discipline featuring
beginning, intermediate, and advanced levels. The training center
now boasts classes on both improv and writing in eight-week terms
and one thousand students go through the program during each
term in Chicago alone.

Once the 1990s began, Second City was about to enter a painful transition. Andrew Alexander hired Kelly Leonard as associate
producer of the Second City Chicago in 1992, essentially usurp-
ing Joyce Sloane from the producer's spot she had held for over
thirty years. Various actors and directors left the Second City in
protest.

The son of a famous Chicago radio personality, Leonard had a
father who knew many of the people in the Chicago entertainment
industry. Deciding he wanted to be a playwright, he had approached his father about entering the Chicago theatre community
somehow, and Roy Leonard gave him the name of Bernie Sahlins,
who was beginning a new theatre company following his sale of
Second City. However, there were still four months before Leonard
could start, so Sahlins referred him to Second City, where Kelly
Leonard joined the bar staff in 1988.

And then, success ensued. As Kelly Leonard described it, "I
showed up on time and got along with people." He also introduced
new facets to the Second City, like sales materials and brochures. He
showed a business savvy that was immediately noticeable. Greater
responsibilities were added to his repertoire until he was eventually
given the job of associate producer in 1992.

That promotion was, as Leonard put it, "a painful, horrible but
ultimately rewarding experience." With the hours and the stress of
the job, Leonard's first marriage fell apart, and the fallout from his
apparent displacing of Joyce Sloane, the longtime producer (who
still remains with the Second City in an advisory and "den mother"
capacity to this day), caused an undeniable amount of stress in the
theatre.

After Sheldon Patinkin directed *Old Wine in New Bottles,* a thirty-fifth-anniversary retrospective revue in 1994, Kelly Leonard became full producer of the Second City, a theatre that was in sore need of revitalization, not only internally but within the rapidly growing improv community, the critics, and the Chicago audiences. Second City's revue format had become so rigid that a class in the training center called "Text Analysis" taught the form of the revue, showing on a scene-by-scene basis all the parts that built a Second City revue. The thing had been around so long that there was very little that strayed from the format.

So, after the theatre looked back and celebrated its thirty-fifth anniversary, 1995 became perhaps the most landmark year in Chicago improvisation since the opening of the Second City. The year began with the ImprovOlympic finally finding a permanent home in Wrigleyville with two stages, giving hundreds of improvisers a new home and providing the theatre with a great deal of press due to catapulted sign-ups to their classes until there were as many as twenty-five teams playing in any given two-month performance schedule.

Second City was a happy recipient of much of the talent that came out of ImprovOlympic, many of whom were utilized in an off-night production called *Lois Kaz,* the first fully improvised production put up by the theatre, a significant event even though the show was relegated to Tuesday nights on the Second City e.t.c. stage, while that resident company performed Wednesdays through Sundays.

Directed by Noah Gregoropoulos, a veteran of ImprovOlympic, *Lois Kaz* united various alumni of Second City's Touring Company and ImprovOlympic, as well as the great, influential ensembles of Ed and Jazz Freddy (both of which we will cover later in the book). Performers included Stephnie Weir, Kevin Dorff, Scott Adsit, Rich Talarico (all of whom would wind up on the Second City Mainstage), and ten others.

"The range of talent," Leonard gushed, "was so wide on that stage and the different styles were really in evidence, because you're talking Dorff, McKay, Koechner, Dratch, Nancy Walls, Scott Adsit . . . They did such beautiful stuff like that opening night, I will never forget, the whole theme of it was about Blake . . . so intellectual, so funny, it was a brilliant show.

"Watching Noah work with them, I have never seen a more gifted improvisational director than Noah at that time . . . I was astounded by his level of insight, the way he worked with those guys, it was masterful."

The show was a huge success and led directly to the creation of the Second City Mainstage's revue *Piñata Full of Bees.* Leonard explains, "I had a yen for the long-form improvisational movement, groups like Ed, Jazz Freddy, going to the IO [ImprovOlympic] fairly frequently, groups like Baron's Barracudas, Blue Velveeta . . . I was into that. And I was a bit of a devotee to Del, even though I'd seen him not have the ability to direct a Second City show during *The Gods Must Be Lazy,* which was horrible."

Leonard continues, "I was very interested in sort of long formers, but when you're starting out in that position [being the new producer], I really was so immersed in detail that I didn't have time to think broadly artistically and I think most of it was intuitive until I had become a little more secure in knowing just what the hell to do on a day-to-day basis."

Leonard and Alexander met with director Tom Gianas and gave him the go-ahead on some unusual casting decisions—that is, unusual to Second City. Leonard explains, "When we were talking about casting the show, Tom had some very specific ideas of people he wanted to bring in that were going to upset the system."

Scott Allman, Scott Adsit, and Jenna Jolovitz had been with the Second City for years and Gianas brought in Jon Glaser and Adam McKay from the e.t.c. stage, and Rachel Dratch straight from the Touring Company, all of whom had been in the cast of *Lois Kaz.* Until that show, popular belief was you made it to the Touring Company, then the e.t.c. stage, and then Mainstage. That belief would be contradicted numerous times over the next six years, with performers like Susan Messing being hired to the Mainstage with no experience on any other Second City stage whatsoever.

Before rehearsals began on *Piñata Full of Bees,* Leonard sat with Tom Gianas and new cast member Adam McKay. "We had lots of discussions about the fact that we wanted to do an all-improvised show, but after a weekend of thinking about it [we dropped the idea]," Leonard said.

"The thing that started to show up early was the tension between the one school of improvisers (Glaser, Dratch, and McKay) and Jenna, Scott, and Scott, you know, more people who were immersed in the Second City system but equally as gifted."

One change was that the improvised sets following the shows during the rehearsal process consisted of Harolds and other long-form pieces. As the show developed, a rock 'n' roll sensibility was apparent, scenes would come back during the course of the show (something rarely seen at Second City), and a certain angry, socially anarchistic attitude permeated the show. One song, "This Is a Song About a Guy in a Wheelchair," was a send-up of the songs Second City had done for years. For years, revues had avoided being too Chicago-centric in an effort not to turn off the myriad tourists who came through the doors, but this show catered more to the local audience. The long-form sensibility of ImprovOlympic veteran Adam McKay was truly the driving force in the revue, which, as the rehearsals progressed, was becoming more of an enormous risk.

Leonard remembers, "I sat through previews that were horrendous. You know, where no one laughed and that was a little scary, but also I think I was young enough then and new enough at the job back then, that I was like, 'Oh, whatever, these guys are funny. They'll be fine.'

"And then on that opening night, I was looking at the critics and they were so shocked at what we did because we hadn't prepared them. We hadn't said anything about it. I didn't know how to do that at the time. They were pretty blown away.

"The most rewarding thing to me was seeing all the people from the community who had written off Second City as being consistently old-hat, as being undaring, were coming in and saying, 'Oh my God! This is the best!' Beyond just being a great show, it revived a spirit inside the building just by being there. It returned the idea of a local audience at Second City, whether those actual numbers changed that much, I don't know. The perception was that we were hip again."

Today there are also more pieces because of the breaking up of longer pieces and spreading them through the show in the form that Del began to explore in *The Gods Must Be Lazy* and that Tom Gianas found the key to in 1995 with *Piñata Full of Bees*.

After *Piñata*, Annoyance Theatre founder Mick Napier directed two wildly successful revues—*Citizen Gates* and *Paradigm Lost*—introducing such ImprovOlympic veterans as Tina Fey, Kevin Dorff, and Stephnie Weir to the stage and creating an equal-gender cast for the first time with the support and encouragement of Leonard.

How did Second City experience its renaissance in the nineties? A lot of it was due to a fresh, creative outlook from a new producer and new directors. Also, a large part of it was the artistic success of ImprovOlympic, considered by many to be the second "Big Daddy" of Chicago's improvisational theatre movement. Del Close and Charna Halpern created a long-form revolution in the 1980s and 1990s that continues unabated today.

What is ImprovOlympic? What made it the one theatre that invites more out-of-towners to Chicago than perhaps any other theatre in Chicago? We will now examine ImprovOlympic and the long form that created a sensation: the Harold.

you couldn't see at Second City or anywhere else. Soon Shepherd moved on and all that was left was the name he had dreamed up. ImprovOlympic lost its format of amateurs and professionals and stuck with just the "professionals," but still the format consisted of the same ten games and the same competition between teams.

The new theatre was in an artistic standstill and Halpern knew she needed a new partner. And she would not remain alone for long. What ImprovOlympic is today is due to the fortuitous arrival of Del Close, who had been fired from Second City (one could best call it a mutual termination) after a ten-year stint as resident director. From 1973 until 1983, Close mentored many of the most famous actors who would come out of the theatre, including John Belushi, Dan Akyroyd, Bill Murray, and others.

When one speaks of improv in Chicago, one has to take a look at the incredibly rich, fascinating life of Del Close. Close's association with improv began with a Compass company begun in St. Louis. In *Something Wonderful Right Away*, Close explains:

> I was seventeen and didn't know shit. I came down to Chicago with a friend—I'd been doing summer stock in Wisconsin— and found an agent. While I was waiting for something to turn up, I took a room in a hotel, and when they discovered I couldn't pay for it, they said, "Well all right, you can start painting hotel rooms." While I was painting hotel rooms, I went to Playwrights and saw a production of *Volpone*. I thought, "This is pretty sleazy but this kind of rings a bell somewhere. These strike me as the kind of people I'd like to work with." I went backstage afterwards, complimenting actors on their performances, and they all walked right by me . . .
>
> Severn [Darden] was down there, and he told me, "There's this action going on in Chicago." The Compass. They were having auditions, so one weekend I took a twin-engine plane up. They had moved twice by that time; they were in the Off-Beat Room on the North Side. (Sweet 1978, 38)

Close credited himself, Elaine May, and Theodore J. Flicker for creating the "rules" of improv that have continued to form the basis of the improv workshops that attract thousands of students in Chicago today. The rules were simple.

1. Don't deny either verbal or physical reality. If you're playing a scene where you're a man and you're on stage with a woman and she states that you two had a child together, you had a child together. Verbally, reality is free to be explored and transformed by both players. If the woman in the scene with you has established there's a coconut on the floor, there's a coconut on the floor. It has been placed there, now and forever, until one of the players makes the choice to move it.

2. The actor's business is to justify. Justification of your partner's action is a primary responsibility of the improviser. Not only must you accept the reality, you are creating the reality together. Why is there a coconut on the floor? Perhaps the wife lied when she said she was on a business trip to Duluth, Minnesota, and in fact spent the time in Tahiti with scantily clad teenage boys. While this may, in the beginning, act as unnecessary exposition, we've established that there are tensions in the marriage. Why did she have to go to Tahiti? It is the business of the improviser playing the husband to justify why she would do such a thing.

Revolutionizing the workshop environment of improvisation was something Close would end up doing time and again. The one stumbling block, however, was his own eccentric behavior. Still, through his travels, Close was a twentieth-century renaissance man, never afraid to experiment with anything: art, drugs, whatever.

For example, after performing with the St. Louis Compass through the end of its run, Close said that he started taking acid for the Air Force in their efforts to investigate REM (rapid eye movement). It wasn't until his role in this experiment ended after an undetermined amount of time that he got a call from one of Second City's cofounders, Howard Alt.

Close was asked that summer to fill in as director while "communication had broken temporarily down between Paul Sills and the company." Second City was not the only thing grabbing Close's attention. One side project that began to gain steam that summer was Close and Severn Darden's Public Cretinization Program, a sort of humorous informal artistic movement they embarked upon to generally poke their noses at people. For example, one of their projects was to try to get the Republicans to nominate Adlai Stevenson since Stevenson's Democratic party had opted to nominate Kennedy.

The program soon ran a contest to see who could come up with the best concept of how to commit suicide. According to Close, his proposed method was to "hang myself from a weather balloon and fly over the city of Los Angeles and as I strangled, my sphincter would relax and I would dribble all over L.A." (Sweet 1978, 145–46). He won.

After leading those summer workshops at Second City, he left to do stand-up comedy, then returned quickly to the theatre in 1962 as a director and performer, beginning a sequence of an on-again, off-again employment that would last for over twenty years.

The first "off" was in 1965, when Close was fired from Second City. Close himself admitted he was high far too often and despite a willing protest of the dismissal by outraged Loyola University students, Close left Second City for San Francisco. He spent the next five years there taking acid and touring with the Merry Pranksters on their famous psychedelic bus. He created light images for the Grateful Dead and recorded a legendary comic album titled *How to Speak Hip*.

Out of all his myriad hippie activities, the most significant improvisational work on the West Coast during this time was his work with the Committee. There he developed a long-form improvisation called the Harold. Committee member Bill Mathieu suggested "Harold" as the name of this form (a la George Harrison naming his haircut "Arthur" in *A Hard Day's Night*) and the name stuck. The name irked Close until the end.

In the beginning workshop days with the Committee, Harold was in somewhat of a raw form. While most improvisation consisted of single scenes, Close thought of the Harold as a sonata form. Themes would be established, a group of characters would return again and again in scenes and then the scenes would work off one another. Different characters would appear in one another's environments. Themes and patterns would emerge and a whole piece would appear in front of the audience's eyes. Close didn't have a particular method by which players could create the Harold. The Harold created itself.

Close would continue to teach the Harold in his workshops at the Committee and at Second City. According to Jonathan Pitts, in these years before ImprovOlympic, the audience suggestion would consist of a question and not just a single word, as would occur at ImprovOlympic in the '80s. Close would continue to utilize the Harold at the Committee and then the Second City in rehearsals for revues as well as the workshops he would host from time to time until he left the theatre for the last time.

Tim Kazurinsky recalls in *Truth in Comedy*, "When we did the Harold back then, we'd take an audience suggestion and line up against the back wall. Alternately, we would begin coming forward in groups of two, starting scenes that really weren't going anywhere yet. Another couple would cut you off or you would fade to the back wall when you were tiring. You would keep this up for 15 or 20 minutes until all these little vignettes began to tie up or interweave" (Close, Halpern, and Johnson 1994, 19).

After directing the Committee for four and a half years, Close felt burned out and returned to Chicago in 1970 and began teaching improv workshops at Kingston Mines Theater Company on Lincoln Avenue. He had brought the Harold with him, opening the eyes of many performers who would go on to greater things. And after a few months of the workshops, he and the students, who would name themselves the Chicago Extension Improv Company, had Sunday-night shows down the street from the Body Politic Theater.

Coincidentally, working at the Body Politic was Paul Sills himself, who had begun new work in Story Theater. During this time, some Second City actors asked Del if he could run some workshops for them while Bernie Sahlins (who had become the company's main director as well as producer and principal owner) was on one of his extended vacations, and they hired him themselves for fifty dollars a shot. Close began teaching workshops and once Sahlins returned from vacation, he gave his blessing to the workshops and asked Close to direct one scene in a new revue, which was a satire of *Hamlet*. The scene was a grand success, perhaps the highlight of the revue. Joyce Sloane offered Del directorship when Del was stranded in Hollywood after Sills dumped his Story Theater actors after an engagement at the Mark Taper Forum. Del directed Second City from 1972 until 1983.

This was the age when Second City actors rose to fame thanks to *SCTV* and *Saturday Night Live*. Close directed many of the most famous faces to grace Chicago's stage, including, of course, John Belushi, Dan Akyroyd, Harold Ramis, Betty Thomas, and many more.

In this, his last and most legendary tenure, Del Close and Second City owner Bernie Sahlins began the legendary argument that would last for over a decade: is improvisation merely a tool to be used in workshops and rehearsals to bring about written material? Or is it an art form in itself, to be presented theatrically in front of a paying audience all by itself? Sahlins believed strongly in the former. Close believed that in order for the Second City to evolve past its tried-and-true tradition, it needed to accept the idea that improv could be performed in front of an audience. After all, Close had taught the Harold for almost fifteen years and seen it succeed in workshops and in front of audiences. Long-form improvisation would work, and people would be willing to pay to see it.

The disagreement became heated enough that Close and Sahlins could no longer work together and Close was fired from Second City in 1983, leaving Sahlins as the sole director until 1988. Not only did Close leave Second City because of the recurring argument, but one other part of his dismissal was his insistence on performing invocations during Second City workshops, according to Jonathan Pitts, who was present during some of them.

According to *Truth in Comedy*, the players in the exercise invoke a group god or demon, which they create themselves from their own group vision. Though Close saw it as an exercise in formulating the group mind, the powers that be at Second City were nonetheless unamused at the theological ramifications of such acts.

ImprovOlympic producer Charna Halpern met Del Close during one of these invocations on Halloween night in 1982 at the Paul Waggoner Art Gallery. Jonathan Pitts recounts: "Those of us who had been doing Del's invocation workshops were doing a performance there that night at 1:30 in the morning. We had a cast of ten. We had twenty-five people in the audience (including Charna), and Del acted as the emcee/witch. He did the opening protection spell. The audience's suggestion for an object to invoke was a watch. It was also the night that the clocks were turned back. I remember because that night on stage in the beginning of the piece I said, 'A lot can happen in an hour that doesn't exist.' Del thought it was a brilliant contribution. It was an excellent show."

Because of her involvement with the erratic David Shepherd, Close had a prejudice against Charna Halpern and their first meeting did not result in the legendary partnership we admire today. Eventually, however, Close left Second City and Halpern needed an infusion of artistic energy in the ImprovOlympic. They met once again, at a bar called CrossCurrents, where she took the chance of offering him the opportunity to teach workshops at her theatre. After weighing her offer and her promise that he could even perform invocations, he accepted.

In 1983, Halpern and Close became partners, and for all intended purposes, the cofounders of the IO we know and love today.

Close also found a new forum in which to teach the Harold, which at the time still did not have a definable structure. Simply, it was a long form that consisted of themes and patterns. There were no rules on where scenes were kept or when games would occur.

One of the games featured in the pre-Close ImprovOlympic was something Halpern called the Time Dash. The Time Dash takes a single important event, like a wedding or a funeral, depending on audience suggestion, and then the audience sees the events occurring before and after the predetermined event. A player might announce, "Six months after the wedding," for example, and we see the bride learn she is pregnant. Another player gets up on stage and announces, "One hour before the wedding," and we see the bride convinced that she shouldn't take the trip to the altar. Et cetera.

Since the ImprovOlympic needed money to survive and it now had under its belt one of the true geniuses of improvisational theatre, Halpern and Close soon devised a way to make the Harold a method they could teach to all levels of improvisers in a series of workshops, from those who had never been on stage before to those who had years of experience at Second City. They combined the Time Dash with the existing idea of Harold and the ImprovOlympic Harold was born.

Halpern and Close were perfect partners: she, a brilliant producer who had an infinite array of survival skills at her disposal and den mother to hundreds of performers, and he, the mad genius. In a recent *Chicago Tribune* article, the difference between Halpern and Close was put best: "Halpern . . . is frequently peppy, always tastefully put together. Close was brilliant, iconoclastic, sloppy, devastatingly dry, and—at least when they met—completely alienated from normalcy, to the point that he refused to have a phone for fear of threatening public officials in a moment of rage. He was, frankly, nuts" (Obejas 2001).

The new, ImprovOlympic version of the Harold is explained in book-length detail in *Truth in Comedy*, but in short, the performers would create a series of three scenes, each with three beats.

The performers would begin with an opening game, consisting of a riffing of that evening's audience suggestion in the form of monologues or repetitions. For example, an audience's suggestion could be "water." The players could each take turns coming out and doing short monologues on any given subject brought to their minds relating to water. Not every monologue would be *about* water, however. The point of the opening in the Harold would be to use that audience suggestion as a starting-off point, from which an endless number of possibilities would emerge to create themes and patterns. The repetitions in some openings would be the players in a semicircle on the stage, each coming up with words inspired by water. Each player would then build on each succeeding word in the pattern. One player says "water," the next says "ocean," the next says "cruise ship," the next says "old people," et cetera. Then, the themes and patterns that emerge in the form that follows could lead off any of those words riffed in the opening.

There are all number of possible opening group games to build off the suggestion, but once that opening completes itself there are three scenes. Then, those three scenes are followed by a group game, we revisit the three scenes at some point in the future (or the past), have another group game, visit the three scenes one last time, and then somehow thematically tie the whole thing together.

This, in an incredibly oversimplified way, was the Harold:

Opening

Scene 1A

Scene 2A

Scene 3A

Group Game 1

Scene 1B

Scene 2B

Scene 3B

Group Game 2

Scene 1C

Scene 2C

Scene 3C

Closing

The Time Dash portion of the Harold could then create a series of rich tapestries for the audience. For example, for the second beat of the first scene, we could see the events carried out six months before the first beat. For the second beat of the *second* scene, we could see events occurring a day following the first beat of the second scene. Eventually, the hope is that somehow in the closing of the piece, the three scenes come together. Often, beginners would forcibly attach the three scenes somehow because that idea is worked into the structure, but the hope is that eventually the closing will unite the scenes organically.

The goal of the structure is to suggest the patterns and themes, whereas in a true Harold, one in which we are not confined by a chart as outlined above, the patterns and themes are created entirely organically. The true test of the performer was following these rules and yet still allowing the themes and patterns to arise organically. Thinking without thinking.

From these organic discoveries comes the group mind. The key to the whole thing is to get to a level of comfort with your fellow players to form a group mind, and the structure just melts away to a point where the Harold becomes something amorphous, much like the somewhat formless long form that Close taught at the Committee and the Second City.

What the new structure brought was the same kind of foothold that Close, Flicker, and May brought when they created the rules at the St. Louis Compass.

By 1984/1985, Close and Halpern had ImprovOlympic and the retooled Harold, and groups were beginning to perform the work on stage in front of a paying audience. The competition between teams that existed in the pre-Close ImprovOlympic remained, but otherwise the transformation was complete. The ImprovOlympic was Halpern and Close's baby. Still, the only missing piece was a permanent location.

It's difficult enough to find a decent space in which to perform in Chicago, but finding a cabaret space, getting the entertainment license, and obtaining the liquor license can take years for any board of directors. However, there was no board of directors. There was only Charna Halpern. It was by sheer willpower that Halpern made the ImprovOlympic survive.

In 1985, the ImprovOlympics took place at a bar in Chicago's Lakeview neighborhood every Tuesday and Saturday night. Rick Kogan of the *Chicago Tribune* wrote an article about a show at Cross-Currents that same year:

> Close opened the proceedings with a typically eclectic, intelligent and barbed 15 minutes in which he managed to hit a dozen topics, from the like of cats to Carl Sagan, "the Barry Manilow of Physics." Then it was on to the first of the three competing teams. In order, these groups of Halpern-Close student-performers were Baron's Barracudas, Apocalypso and Pigwings. After being given a theme by audience suggestion, each group proceeded to explore it by means of such improvisational techniques as time dashes, monologues, musical spots and split scenes. At the conclusion of each group's set, roughly 40 minutes long, the group was graded by the audience on a 1–6 scoring system in four categories—intelligence, theme, structure and teamwork.

This was a fairly complex task to ask of an audience in a bar, but, as Kogan describes, many of the audience members were already well acquainted with the casts:

> It was surprising that so many people—one of the largest crowds in the history of [CrossCurrents]'s cabaret— . . . on the other hand, perhaps it's not really that surprising. When there are 20-some performers and each of them asks a few friends to "come on by and see me on stage Saturday night," large crowds will ensue.

Soon, more than just the performers' friends were aware of the ImprovOlympic. In December 1986, George D. Miller, the secretary general of the U.S. Olympic Committee, sent Halpern and Close a letter "threatening legal action if Halpern and Close did not at once cease using the Olympic name in connection with their endeavor" (Kogan 1987). ImprovOlympic did point out that they were involved in the *improvisational theatre* business and had no desire to steal the luster of the Olympics' name. After all, there was little confusing an improv comedy theatre with an international sporting event. Still, the Olympics pressed on in their fight for intellectual property. For a while, the theatre was renamed ImprovOlympia until an agreement was reached that would allow the use of the name ImprovOlympic until 2002, at which point the theatre's name becomes IO.

Another major event in 1986 was when actor-producer Michael Douglas read an article about ImprovOlympic in the *New York Times*. He decided to try to put together a television show featuring the Harold. Chris Beard, creator of the *Gong Show* and *Putting on the Hits,* came to see the show and negotiations dragged on for about a year before a pilot was made. Featuring Del and Charna as referees overseeing various improv games, the show would feature celebrity judges in place of the audiences that would see the shows live on stage. Unfortunately, as often happens with bigwigs from the networks, various complications ensued. The network decided that Halpern's handpicked performers (who included David Koechner and Noah Gregoropoulos) were not up to snuff and hired instead "dick joke" comics who were completely unsuitable. Naturally, with the untalented performers going up instead of the talented ones Halpern chose, the pilot was not as funny as people had hoped. The network naturally did not put the blame on the performers *they* had chosen.

Still, despite the setback, ImprovOlympic continued its steady growth in reputation. In 1987 a show from the ImprovOlympic came to CrossCurrents called *Honor Finnegan Versus the Brain of the Galaxy,* a collaboration between Close and members of the Harold team Baron's Barracudas, which is regarded as the first great Harold team at ImprovOlympic. The namesake of the title was Honor Finnegan, who had won an amateur saloon singer's contest at That Steak Joynt, a restaurant that stood for years next door to Second City. It was the first written show presented by ImprovOlympic.

"Imagine Little Orphan Annie playing the Sigourney Weaver role in *Aliens,* and you'll have some idea of the show," said Close. "It explores such issues as the extinction of life on earth, the threat of alien invasion, life after death, the loneliness of heroism. Bad taste being used to good ends." Commenting on the show, Close added, "I could never have done something like this at Second City. I couldn't do a play, except in the old days" (Kogan 1987).

Oddly enough, in two years, Close would return to Second City to direct one more revue, until which point, ImprovOlympic thrived at CrossCurrents until the owner of the place skipped town and it was bought out by James Cotton, who converted the place into a blues club called Cotton Chicago. ImprovOlympic and Metraform (who performed upstairs and about whom we'll learn more in the next chapter) continued to perform until August 1989, when Cotton Chicago closed.

ImprovOlympic looked like it was finished and Second City invited Close to direct his first revue in seven years. He took time off from teaching and then promptly fired most of the cast from the previous revue, bringing in future *SNL* stars Chris Farley and Tim Meadows and attempting to implement many Harold techniques into the show, mostly that of Halpern's Time Dash, revisiting scenes seen earlier in the revue.

Second City was entering its fourth decade and the accusations were beginning that the Wells Street landmark had become only that—a landmark. The revue was the most poorly received in recent memory and although it gave Farley and Meadows a well-deserved start, Close quickly lost interest in the show and he never worked for Second City again.

Fortunately, Halpern's fortitude paid off. Homeless for nearly a year, ImprovOlympic reopened on June 22, 1990, in the basement at Papa Milano at 1970 North Lincoln Avenue. With relatively new owners, the venue had previously had the distinction of being owned by former Bears quarterback Jim McMahon. The basement would now house 150 seats, what Halpern called "the comedy cellar" with "the perfect ambience for improvisation" (Kogan 1990).

That same year, ImprovOlympic ran The Southern Comfort Team Comedy Challenge, a national search for the best improvisational comedy team in the country. Close and Halpern conducted workshops in six cities, from which the teams would be chosen to compete in regional contests. The official spokesman was IO and Second City alumnus Mike Myers, who had just begun his wildly successful run on *Saturday Night Live*. The challenge was very successful and helped IO's status grow even more, as well as the growing fame of Myers and fellow alumnus on *SNL,* Chris Farley. ImprovOlympic had been around long enough to boast of celebrities originating there.

ImprovOlympic moved several more times until 1993, when they ended up occupying a fairly stable storefront location on West Belmont Avenue, as well as a bar just a few doors down from Wrigley Field, called the Wrigleyside. For a couple of years, ImprovOlympic occupied both places, a smart move considering Halpern and Close's experience with the instability of spaces.

In 1993, ImprovOlympic reached another pinnacle when their house team the Family performed in a critically acclaimed improvised production called *Three Mad Rituals.* The Family was Matt Besser, Ian Roberts, Ali Fahrahnakian, Miles Stroth, Neil Flynn, and Adam McKay, a group that Del Close realized had infinite potential. The show consisted of three forms taught at the ImprovOlympic: the Deconstruction, the Movie, and the Harold, all coming from a single suggestion of a line of poetry at the beginning of the evening. It became perhaps the archetypal ImprovOlympic show, with the Family becoming what some called "the greatest team in the world." They essentially created for performance the Deconstruction and the Movie. Also, the team spawned the careers of Besser and Roberts, who became half of the Upright Citizens Brigade, and McKay, who would become head writer of *Saturday Night Live.*

And while great things were happening at the Wrigleyside, Halpern and Close were still searching for a facility where they could have their *own* bar. Just two doors north of Wrigleyside was a building that would soon provide a suitable home for ImprovOlympic—at long last. In March 1995 Halpern and Close opened a theatre with two stages. The Harold Cabaret, housed in the basement with a full bar, would showcase the teams formed from the growing workshops provided by Del and Charna. Upstairs stood the Del Close Theater, with one hundred seats provided by the recently demolished Chicago Stadium in a more proscenium-based setting (but still with a bar, albeit a partial one). The upstairs theatre would be devoted to plays, more experimental improv outside the realm of the Harold shows, and would be rented out to outside theatres.

The improv explosion in Chicago went nuclear. Now that ImprovOlympic had a permanent home, the theatre quickly gained more notoriety and a greater presence in the Chicago theatre scene. Another important development was the publication of *Truth in Comedy* (1994), cowritten by Halpern and Close with Kim "Howard" Johnson, a former student of theirs who has since become rightfully known as the world expert on Monty Python. *Truth in Comedy* provided the guidebook to the long-form philosophy that Halpern and Close had formulated over the past twelve years, showing readers worldwide how to look for the game in the scene, how to keep an open mind, how to start in the middle, and how to follow many other rules that have become necessities for long-form improvisation.

Students of improvisation nationwide now had access to the Harold without the necessity of flying Close and Halpern out for a workshop. Thus, students flocked from around the country to Chicago, not to try to make it at Second City, but to study with Del Close. Often, making it to Second City was the larger goal since it had had twenty more years to produce famous people than ImprovOlympic did.

Then, the astounding critical and popular success of Second City's revue *Piñata Full of Bees* was in many ways ImprovOlympic's ultimate victory and Close's final retribution at the theatre whose legend he helped build.

Ironically, in 1978, Close had said, "You know, at the beginning, in Compass and the first days of Second City, we had a definite sense of being part of the process of history in the making—hanging ten out in the front of something forging away into the unknown. Now, to some degree, the thrill of discovery is gone" (Sweet 1978, 156).

He found out that the thrill of the discovery was far from over.

Through the Harold, ImprovOlympic made standard many conventions that we see in long-form improvisation today.

*Truth in Comedy* goes through the steps of becoming a successful Harold performer. Some of the advice the authors give is true brilliance in its simplicity and gives definition to improvisation that did not exist before. Most of the terms and phrases that improv students in Chicago hear today come directly from Harold.

## Edits

In long form, scenes are not broken apart by audience suggestions, so the players need to decide when to begin and end scenes. The simplest and most popular of these edits is the sweep edit, in which the player simply walks across the stage, upstage of the scene. Another move, which is less popular, is the whoosh edit, which is just like a sweep edit, except the player spreads his arms like wings and says, "Whoosh."

Over the course of long-form improvisation shows throughout the years, Close and other directors have worked on more seamless transitions between scenes to lend more of a visual unity between scenes. For example, a player may enter a scene with a strong initiation, making it obvious that she is not entering the previous scene.

## The Game in the Scene

While scenic improvisation is not game oriented, there are still games within those scenes, games that—if played at the height of your intelligence—can make great comedy.

## Show, Don't Tell

This applies to all visual arts. Rather than talk about going to the quarry to find dinosaur eggs, it's far more interesting to the audience members and your fellow players if you actually go to the quarry. After all, with object work and your ability to manipulate your environment on stage any way you like, there is no reason to talk about something when you can just go there.

## Rule of Threes

The narrative arc of traditional storytelling requires a beginning, a middle, and an end—three parts of the whole. From this, the magic of the rule of threes originates. The Harold itself is composed of three beats in each of three scenes, separated into three different portions. Three is everywhere. It's in our storytelling blood.

## Present Action

This is one of the more important basic rules taught to beginning improvisers. In Harold especially, when you have two to three minutes to devote to a beat of a scene at a time, the action must always move forward. Other forms, like the Deconstruction, don't rely so much on fast, forward action, but it's still a true rule that belongs in the improv bible.

## Silence

This is one of the long-form improvisation tenants that can be very hard to accomplish in a noisy cabaret or bar environment, where many improv shows end up in Chicago. The greatest Harold teams know when to shut up! If you need to explore your environment or let something your partner said sink in, let it. This ideal alone separates some fine, intelligent long-form work from work that is simply stand-up with more than one person on stage.

## The Group Mind

Truly, the development of the group mind was one of the revolutionary gifts that ImprovOlympic gave theatre. There's something awe inspiring, mysterious, magic about Harold that unites players into a common storytelling goal. A truly tested team no longer feels the hesitation of speaking up for fear of interrupting someone.

ImprovOlympic also established the crimes of improvisation. Asking questions is a big no-no. Rather than ask, tell. Or even better than tell, show.

Character motivation is crucially important in a Harold. One of the most important points that Halpern makes in *Truth in Comedy* is to react honestly. Improvisers deny this simple lesson every night in Chicago, while the ones who move on to greatness are more concerned with what their characters are saying rather than what accent they're throwing at it.

There are, of course, many other steps in becoming a successful improviser at ImprovOlympic. The theatre continues to grow. It was operating with an annual budget of $600,000 in 1995; in five years it had grown to $850,000. A brand-new facility housing IO West opened in Los Angeles in the spring of 2001, a facility so impressive and grand that it seemed necessary to find a new home for the host theatre in Chicago. IO Chicago needs a theatre as grand as its reputation, and so work is being done to expand to a beautiful four-floor complex.

Del Close died in March 1999 from complications of emphysema, which had slowly hindered his ability to even climb the stairs to the theatre that Halpern had named after him four years earlier. Still, he went with the kind of style that only a proud instigator of the Public Cretinization Program would go. He held a farewell party from his hospital bed in the waning days of his life, a party attended by loyal students past and present including Harold Ramis and Bill Murray, which was televised soon afterward on Comedy Central. And of course, the coup de grace: the willing of his own skull to the Goodman Theatre so he could play Yorick in any future productions of *Hamlet* that the theatre might stage. Halpern went through hell trying to get Close's final wish honored and finally managed to get the deal done. The now-legendary skull is now in possession of the Goodman to use as they will.

Despite Close's passing, plenty of loyal students and teachers continue to nurture the Harold and all of Del Close's teachings. Close had instigated a performance class near the end of his life, in which the top-level classes were able to create forms of their own and those classes continue under the tutelage of Noah Gregoropoulos. Baby Wants Candy became the first resident team in IO history several years ago, joining the likes of the Family and Baron's Barracudas as a legendary team, but with its own unique twist on improv: creating a completely improvised musical three times a week.

There is a kind of intense family commitment present at IO that showed at the theatre's two-night twentieth-anniversary reunion in August 2001, in which nearly everyone alive who had become successful in due part to Charna Halpern and Del Close came and

*Figure 3–1: Charna Halpern* Photo by Suzanne Plunkett

performed once more. An introduction by IO manager Peter Gwinn let the audience know that in order to eliminate confusion between the Olympics and their theatre, the name IO would be the new name of the theatre. However, in a celebration of the theatre's twenty years, today's audiences were able to see once again the legendary teams like Blue Velveeta and the Family. It was a magical moment.

The future of IO Chicago and IO West is certainly a rosy one. Halpern and her teachers continue to foster young improvisers, many of whose pictures will hang on the wall beside the faces of Farley, Myers, Tina Fey, Rachel Dratch, Amy Poehler, and the hundreds of other improvisers who have had the honor of performing on the ImprovOlympic stage.

The Harold still lives as a launching point for hundreds of young improvisers who wish to express themselves on stage. While none of them will have the distinct pleasure of learning under Del Close, there are plenty of people carrying the torch into the twenty-first century.

# **4**  The Torchbearers

ven before ImprovOlympic became world famous through its
revolutionary approach to long-form improvisation, students
who had studied there wished to adapt their love of improvisation into their own words.

As the popularity of ImprovOlympic skyrocketed during the
'80s and '90s, Charna Halpern and Del Close could not have antici-
pated the volume of theatre companies devoted to improvisation
that would sprout up over the next fifteen years in the city of Chicago and around the country. As covered earlier, Halpern and Close
proved that you can create an entire evening's entertainment out of
purely improvised material through their teaching of the Harold.
Despite a gypsylike existence traveling from bar to bar in the '80s—
even closing up shop for nearly a year—the company enjoyed wide-
spread popularity. In the early '90s they found a theatre space in
Lakeview and by 1995 finally established a permanent location
three doors away from Wrigley Field.

As a result of the theatre blossoming over the course of its first
decade, more performers than ever before were benefiting from improvisational training. One of the primary reasons so many students
of improv eagerly flocked to IO was the guarantee that you would
get real stage time in front of audiences as a result of your training.

Halpern would teach the introductory classes and surmise which students worked best with which students and form teams usually consisting of anywhere from six to eleven players. Those teams would get stage time, sometimes continuing at the theatre for years while others would have short lives, based on Halpern and Close's judgment on whether the team would have any potential on their stage.

The logic behind this system was brilliant. By luring students to their program and promising them stage time, there was a guaranteed audience for every show. New performers would inevitably invite all their friends and family to performances, and while the new teams were often less than spectacular, Halpern could pair them in a program with an experienced team who, more often than not, had perfected the Harold to such a degree that no matter how poor the first team performed, they'd make the show successful. Audiences who enjoyed the second team would come back for more. It was this kind of savvy thinking that helped Improv-Olympic thrive.

Even as the theatre was struggling, Halpern had perfected the art of the sell. Approaching a bar owner with the question "Want to make some money?" the system as it began would give the ImprovOlympic ostensibly free rent while the bar would collect all the drink receipts. From the bar owner's perspective, it was the perfect alternative to paying live bands. He didn't have to pay ImprovOlympic a penny, and he would collect all the beer money, which at the beginning would often consist primarily of performers' purchases. However, the economic reality of owning a bar in Chicago, where rent and property taxes increase at a seemingly infinite rate, was that the beer swilling by the improvisers was often simply not enough.

Once alumni like Chris Farley and Mike Myers made a name for themselves on *Saturday Night Live,* ImprovOlympic was able to feed on the same curiosity level that attracted audiences to the famous-alumni-heavy Second City.

There is a certain irony that ImprovOlympic thrives on the fame of its former students and has become a second-generation Second City, and one wonders if that irony was likely not lost on the late Del Close. Black-and-white photos of old teams now adorn the theatre, much like the photos on the walls of Second City, and wistful stories of days gone by permeate the halls.

After the success of ImprovOlympic, improv groups in Chicago saw their chance to follow in Close and Halpern's footsteps. A model had been created. Chicago was the kind of town where theatre companies could get started with relatively little expense. Storefront theatres that littered the north side of the city, accompanied by hopeful stories of how Gary Sinise and Steppenwolf had started their theatre in a basement in Highland Park, were filled with the hopes and dreams of scores of actors who had come to Chicago expressly to become the next big comic star.

In Chicago, there is little or no money to be made in theatre but this is simply an accepted way of life. The goal of many actors coming to Chicago is to gain enough experience to go to Los Angeles and New York armed with a fat resume and ready to work. But what of the actors and improvisers who had no wish to go to L.A. or New York? What of those who simply loved their work and loved to be in Chicago?

These were hundreds of improvisers, eager to continue their work. Not every improv theatre that sprouted in the next fifteen years came directly from IO, but many of them would not have happened if not for Halpern and Close.

Since all these improvisers could not fit into one theatre, they either formed their own theatres or became roving improv groups that would perform anywhere they could. In this chapter, we will cover some of these theatres that have become successful.

There are many improv theatres throughout the country that have used ImprovOlympic as an inspiration but there is simply not enough room in this volume to include them all. Not taking anything against groups and theatres in other cities, but the amazing diversity of the performers and theatres in Chicago deserves a chapter on its own and for brevity's sake, we must skip the entire rest of the country. Unfair, perhaps, but understandable once one realizes the scope of talent that resides in the Windy City.

## Metraform and the Annoyance Theater

The Annoyance Theater was built from an association that began between the principal founders at Indiana University in the early 1980s. Students Mick Napier and David McFarland read *Something Wonderful Right Away* (Sweet 1978), saw a Second City show in Chicago, and decided they had learned enough about the work from the book and the single show to start up their own improv group at Indiana. The group was called Dubbletaque (pronounced "doubletake") and original members included Joe Bill, Mark Henderson, and others. Once Henderson graduated, Napier, Bill, and company brought in Mark Sutton. They performed Second City–style revues, using improvisation in workshops as the basis for college-oriented sketch comedy. It was a trial by fire, writing a new revue every two weeks in an attempt to make 150 drunk frat boys laugh on a consistent basis. None of them, before reading Sweet's book, had ever seen an improv show or taken an improv class. They depended entirely on what had influenced them previously.

Mick Napier recalls, "Monty Python influenced me, *Saturday Night Live* influenced me just as far what sketch comedy was or could be. So the group we had, we did mostly a sketch show, in bars and stuff in Indiana, Bloomington, and then we'd do improv. It was all games. I don't think we ever really improvised a scene unless a scene was part of the game. I didn't even really know about scenic improvisation at that point."

"What turned me on about [improv]," he continues, "was, like, I could get the same performance fix without having to go through all the work of rehearsing, pretty much. And then other things . . . it was just fun to be funny, spontaneous. Later, when I moved to Chicago, what turned me on about it was the entire scene, the social aspects of it, the whole culture of it was a lot of fun to me.

"We were rather naïve because we thought we could write a new show, a new hour sketch show every week, and we did. And most of it worked . . . and I look back at that and think about the amount of time it takes to put a Mainstage show up at Second City [and] it kinda makes me laugh. Relative perspective, I guess."

Once Napier got to Chicago, he took classes at ImprovOlympic and joined a team called Grime and Punishment, which included future *SNL* star Tim Meadows. After doing that for a while, Napier recalls, "the side of me that started Metraform was kind of in reaction to being relegated to one kind of improv form at IO at the time, the Harold. And wanting to explore different kinds of forms, different kinds of things and also the altruist in me that's really not worked for me in my life, what I wanted to allow was a lot of different people to improvise a lot of different things.

"Metraform's early days made me very cynical about forms and I'll tell you why: it's because we had one group of people that liked to improvise together, that performed at the Cabaret Metro on the fourth floor.

"Then there was another thing that I organized, which was about having different people coach different forms—dozens of forms—and performed them at a place called the Clout Club, which became Lounge Ax, and we would do four or five different forms a week. And one of my favorites was Dave Pasquesi led a séance as an improv form. . . . It became very clear then that you can sit down and think of ten new forms in about an hour.

"And I became very cynical of anyone that placed any importance on a new form and had it be a revelation . . . so when the Movie came out at IO, like *okay* . . . there are dozens and dozens and dozens."

The ensemble soon moved to the upstairs space at CrossCurrents (where the ImprovOlympic did shows downstairs) and had a hit show with *Splatter Theater.* Napier decided to put up a show consisting of every single horror movie cliché in the book. The stage was dressed white, the actors wore white, and there was enough fake blood that, according to Mark Sutton, when the space was renovated by a different owner nearly a decade later, the workers had to spend much of their time scraping the old fake blood from the floors.

Adapting Second City's formula of improvising in rehearsal, the Metraform shows employed the director as both director and head writer. Mark Sutton explains, when Napier conceived their breakthrough hit *Co-Ed Prison Sluts,* he gave the following information to the cast: "Here's the deal. It's a musical, set in prison, it's going to be vulgar and there's going to be a scene where a clown will fight a guy dressed as a woman. That's all I know."

Napier says, "I remember teaching a class at Second City and writing down *Co-Ed Prison Sluts* and then showing that to the class, and saying 'That's a good name for a play!'"

The method of development and rehearsal that Napier and company employed was a cross between the Compass' scenario play and the Second City revue. While a very sketchy outline is made up for a show, there are still many more blanks to fill in. Some Annoyance shows had more structure than others. A prime example of more of a sense of structure is *The Real Live Brady Bunch,* which, along with *Co-Ed,* put the Annoyance Theater on the map.

Subsequent to the owner-switching drama at CrossCurrents covered last chapter, Napier and his fellow Metraform players decided to go it alone, foregoing the free rent at unreliable bars and signing a five-year lease at a former drag bar on Broadway just south of Belmont Street in Chicago, a lease that Sutton explains "was a mistake." Their inexperience with real estate got them stuck at a storefront property where they ended up having to pay the majority of property taxes. Still, thanks to *Co-Ed Prison Sluts, The Real Live Brady Bunch,* and other shows, the new theatre was a success. Problem was, the theatre needed a name. Metraform wasn't going to cut it, so after rejecting names like Unlucky Pets Theater and Le Ping Pong Theater, Metraform's Annoyance Theater was born. Soon "Metraform" was cut out entirely.

About a year and a half after the Annoyance Theater opened, they started teaching classes, not only improv but also scene study and other "normal" acting classes. Mick Napier had been teaching at the Second City Training Center, then the Joyce Sloane controversy ensued and Napier decided perhaps he should teach classes at the Annoyance, making money for his own theatre. Workshops with a theatrical bent, concentrating on movement and voice, were the norm to begin with, but soon the Annoyance became known as the third of the "Big Three" when discussing where someone should study improv.

While *Co-Ed Prison Sluts* wasn't always the focus of the Annoyance Theater, it ran for eleven years, becoming its cash cow Friday and Saturday nights at 10:30, allowing for experimentation on other evenings. Says Mark Sutton, "We always wanted to be a place to go up on stage and have the freedom to suck and nobody would care. We've put up shows that are bad, so we can learn without fear of retribution." *Co-Ed* finally closed in June of 2000 because, according to Sutton, the expectation had become that every Annoyance show would be just like *Co-Ed* and they didn't want that conception to exist anymore.

The Annoyance teachers, such as Napier, Joe Bill, and Susan Messing, practiced a form of improvisation that could best be described as subversive. The key stylistic choice in improvisers who have come from the Annoyance is to just get out there on stage and start saying something, *anything,* immediately. Other long-form performers often use their first moment on stage to plant themselves in an environment, exhibiting object work, sometimes studying their partner. The Annoyance style rejected this practice. Rather than making any conscious decision when first planting himself on stage, the performer is encouraged to say whatever comes to his mind without consciously thinking it.

This practice can be misinterpreted by performers who merely use the technique to yell and swear. Again, this can be blamed on the expectation that the teachers wanted *Co-Ed Prison Sluts* to be re-created on their stage in workshops. What they didn't realize was that the Annoyance's style depended not on the shock value of its rather raw approach, but on the immediacy of every word put there on stage. If the performer caught himself off guard, certainly the audience would absorb that immediate emotion, augmenting the audience's voyeuristic thrill in seeing things as they happened.

The huge bills caused by the Broadway space's awful lease precipitated another move. This time, hardened by the experience of being pushed around by a landlord, they got a real estate agent and found the space on Clark, across the street from the Metro, in 1994. Long an abandoned warehouse, the new theatre boasted twice the space of the original theatre and was second only to Second City in the amount of usable space in the theatre and in the basement.

Eventually, the Annoyance's Clark Street space closed in June 2000. However, the lack of a permanent venue was far from the end of the theatre. It still produced shows by renting other theatre space around the North side and teaching classes; the closing of the Clark Street space harkened a new chapter in the Annoyance's history. It was due not only to outside forces closing the space but also a decision on the part of Mick Napier to move on.

Napier says, "When the owner of the building we were renting decided to sell the building, it was not an unhappy piece of information for me. For a couple of years, I thought I was in a grind at the Annoyance. While we did occasionally good shows, I thought we were slipping in what we did and all that. So I was kind of happy, I saw it as an opportunity. When we were offered the same deal by the new owner for a while, I refused it because I wanted that to be something that would put the Annoyance at stake, put me at stake again. It's now been over a year since we've had a theatre. In that year, we've written a business plan, wanting to get financing for a production company that would include a training program, a production facility, and a theatre. I really feel like the time is really good for the opportunity to have a production studio in Chicago that can utilize all the vast comedy resources here and actually reduce film, television, and any other kind of medium that exists on this digital planet right now.

"It is very tough battle," says Napier. "The financial sector in Chicago doesn't understand the entertainment industry at all. The venture capital world is completely dead thanks to the tech industry and the economy, so that's a rough road.

"Chicago itself has a mentality that is enamored by celebrity and it doesn't seem to want to own it in its own city. They'd rather talk about it afar rather than propagate it here. The talent pool is also in a lot of ways like that. Everyone is saying the words, 'We wanna do this here,' but no one really believes it. It's a weird thing. From casting directors to agents—agents jump through hoops in this city if something's going to happen in New York or Los Angeles. That's what I'm trying to get through. I'm going to give it all I can to get through that and create such a place here. It's what I'd like to do."

While the Annoyance approaches another step in its evolution, Napier looks back. "I think the Annoyance has always been kind of disregarded insofar as the markets left in the evolution of improvisation because of the content of the Annoyance. The content is trashy quite often, but we're really taking from the Compass Players in a way to develop an entire full-length play by utilizing improvisation. I feel very proud of the Annoyance in that it did utilize improvisation to create over ninety works that were full length—not all of those used that process. I would say sixty, and for the good or the bad in the way of content, we were very prolific in believing you could take improvisation and create a full play. And I think that's overshadowed sometimes by the Annoyance's content."

In January 2002, Annoyance Productions opened their production space on Lincoln Avenue in Chicago, realizing Napier's dream. Consisting of 3,800 square feet devoted to rehearsal space and film and video production, the Annoyance's production space would prove again the company's resilience and drive. What the future holds may be limitless.

*Figure 4–1: Jazz Freddy* Photo by Suzie Gardner

## Jazz Freddy

Perhaps the most legendary improv group of the early '90s along with the Family, during the time when ImprovOlympic really began flowering, Jazz Freddy was an independent ensemble made up of IO performers and other improvisers. They did not start their own theatre but they influenced so many other improvisers during this time period that they might as well have built a bricks-and-mortar institution.

Brian Stack, now a writer on *Late Night with Conan O'Brien,* was a member of Jazz Freddy. He had become interested in improv at Indiana University, where the first improv he ever saw was performed by Mick Napier's group Dubbletaque.

He recalls, "Pete Zarahdnik had been involved in the group ED, which had been very successful doing long-form improv in places like the Remains Theater. He had also been involved with some of the rest of us at ImprovOlympic and, later, in a drunken joke of a group called Gambrinus, King of Beer, which performed at [a place called] At the Tracks.

"When ED finished up, Pete pulled some of us from Gambrinus and put us together with some of his ED friends. The initial Jazz Freddy cast included Pete, Susan MacLaughlin, Stephanie Howard, Meredith Zinner, Miriam Tolan, Chris Reed, Jimmy Carrane, Kevin Dorff, Noah Gregoropolous, David Koechner, me, Pat Finn, and Rachel Dratch. . . . We also had lots of guest performers sitting in during the run, like Dave Pasquesi, Brian McCann, Chris Hogan, Theresa Mulligan, and Lauren Katz. They would usually sit in one at a time."

Noah Gregoropoulos was already a veteran at ImprovOlympic, a former fellow cast member of Gambrinus, King of Beer, and a member of Jazz Freddy. "We just basically got together not even to put a show up. It was 'We want to reinvest in patient, reality-based scenework.' We basically just got together in the Live Bait Theater, where we acted scenes for each other without the idea of putting up a show. Then it developed into a show as a result of that and it was extremely popular. It's really where sort of the Monday-night phenomena started, you know, you could really get a lot of actors to come to your show if you have your show on a Monday night."

Gregoropoulos says, "We basically sold the place out every show. We had to turn people away. We got national press in places like the *American Theater* magazine. It got so much critical attention that it sort of caused other places around town, especially the ImprovOlympic, where at that time just had the Harold schedule, Del saw basically what was going on, he had these incredibly talented people not being asked to push it beyond what they were already doing, so the Family was together at the time, so he said, 'Let's do a show with the Family.'" The result was *Three Mad Rituals,* in many ways a show that made ImprovOlympic turn the corner and become successful enough for IO to get a permanent home.

Before that, however, Jazz Freddy worked hard to get the attention they received. Stack recalls, "The Jazz Freddy rehearsal process was by far the most time-consuming and intensive one I'd ever been involved with up to that point. We rehearsed four or five nights a week, I think, for around three hours at a time. I could be wrong, but I think we kept a pretty intense rehearsal schedule for the months after the show opened as well. Before Jazz Freddy, most of the 'rehearsing' I'd done involved getting together once a week or so with my team and our coach at IO, or sitting around socializing with friends, telling ourselves we were 'rehearsing.' It was fun but not too productive."

Noah Gregoropoulos also recalls the rehearsal process. "That's something that I've never experienced anything like in an improv show since Jazz Freddy, was the amount of rehearsing that went on.

"By the second run we had the kind of commitment that isn't there for any show I've seen, or been involved in, even shows I've directed," says Gregoropoulos. "You can't get people together three and four times a week and abandon all other things they're working on. That's basically what we did. I mean literally! Dave Koechner turned down a [Second City] Touring Company gig, or delayed it, to commit to the rehearsal process of Jazz Freddy. Pete Gardner got Miller Beer to move a national commercial shoot so that he wouldn't miss rehearsals for Jazz Freddy. A *national commercial shoot!* That absolutely won't happen. People won't miss a Playground show to rehearse for an IO show *now*."

Brian Stack remembers, "Our rehearsals usually started with an extensive warm-up. Early on, the former IO people in Jazz Freddy were a little impatient with that, I think, but we didn't complain and it ended up being very beneficial to us. We did a lot of physical warm-ups like stretching, etc. Even mild stretching for me is a considerable challenge since I have the flexibility of a Carolina oak. When we'd get into the scenework, all the warm-up stuff would pay off. I think we were more focused and appreciative of the scene time since we hadn't just jumped into it at the start of rehearsal.

"One moment I remember very well was during a show we did on Halloween night, '92. We decided to wear costumes but made it a rule not to play characters that one would associate with those costumes. For example, Kevin Dorff was dressed as Hugh Hefner but didn't play Hefner in any of the scenes. Carlos Jacott was dressed as a cartoonish Mexican bandito with a huge sombrero, eye patch, big bushy mustache, boots, guns, and bullets draped across his chest. In one scene, however, he was playing a typical little American boy who had just returned from Little League practice. Jimmy Carrane, who was playing Carlos' dad, told him, 'Take that hat off in the house, young man.' Rather than taking off the ridiculously large sombrero he was wearing, Carlos reached up a pulled off a pantomimed little boy's baseball cap. It brought the house down, but maybe you had to be there.

"I remember one night in which Kevin Dorff was receiving messages from Satan on his answering machine. That was a really fun recurring bit. Why Satan communicated that way was never fully made clear, but the crowd loved it. I also remember in one rehearsal when Dave Koechner first did his Gerald Tibbins character, a character he later did on *SNL* and will soon be the subject of a movie. It was an instant classic, one of the funniest and most original characters I've ever seen anyone do—a white-trash guy with incredible arrogance and yet somehow really likable, too. We were all looking at each other as if to say, 'Where the hell did he come up with *this* one?'"

When recalling exactly what sort of form Jazz Freddy attempted, Stack remembers, "As Craig Cackowski (who came to a lot of our shows, God bless him) said so accurately, the Jazz Freddy show was more about content than form but there was a structure you could learn if you wanted to. The form would basically start with two people whom Pete had assigned to start the show. They would do a two-person scene taking off from the audience's suggestion. Then, we would start into what we called a 'two-back, one-forward' sequence. By that, I mean that someone would come in and tag out one of the characters from the first scene and take the remaining person back in time. That could mean many years back in time or a few minutes.

"For example, if the first scene involved an abusive dad and his son, the next actor coming in might tag out the son and start the next scene as a long-ago scene involving the abusive dad as a child, dealing with a school bully or his own abusive dad. Or, the actor coming in could tag out the dad and take the son back in time to twenty minutes earlier at school where the son bullies other kids the way his dad bullies him. The third scene would again feature a 'back-in-time' tag, removing one of the actors from the second scene. The fourth scene would involve a 'forward' tag in which one of the actors would then be taken *ahead* in time. After that, for the first act, the form was wide open. In the second act, the form would start exactly as it did in the first. The first act would feature about half of the cast and the second act would feature the other half, usually. Then, if I'm remembering correctly, there was a third act in which everyone was out there, often calling back characters and relationships that were established in the first and second acts.

Throughout all three acts, the two-person scenes could, of course, be added onto by walk-ons from other cast members or by whole new characters entering and playing major roles in the scenes.

"It might sound more complicated than it was. The bottom line was really just trying to do the best scenework we could do.

"I think that, in the end, the focus was on doing really good scenework and I think that, on most nights, we succeeded at that. We all individually had off-nights and on-nights but our group had such good chemistry and such a mix of performance styles that there was usually something special in every show. And, on some nights, everything came together and we really surprised ourselves. The best nights we had were as fun and rewarding as anything I've ever been a part of."

Stack says, "I don't think we necessarily broke a lot of new ground with Jazz Freddy. We really just tried to do the best scenework we could do. I think that any influence the group may have had came from the fact that the shows were usually patient and funny, and that they were performed in a theatre environment as opposed to a bar. Also, we were lucky enough to get attention from the press, which always helps get the word out and, let's face it, the press can have a great impact."

After two more runs of shows, Jazz Freddy walked into the improv sunset. Many of the performers in Jazz Freddy went on to star in the Second City e.t.c. show called *Lois Kaz,* which introduced long-form improvisation to a Second City stage and set the theatre up for their revue *Piñata Full of Bees* in 1995. Then, the group members went their separate ways, all reaching the heights of success. Many went on to *Saturday Night Live* or *Late Night with Conan O'Brien,* or simply found their way to Los Angeles or New York. People still talk about Jazz Freddy today. Whether or not another group can come along with their kind of commitment is in some doubt, but people hope.

## The Free Associates

A nonprofit theatre founded in 1991, the Free Associates have rather uniquely stayed comfortably outside the inner long-form circle of which ImprovOlympic is the center. A veteran improviser named Mark Gagne began the troupe with a focus on improvised parody. The troupe's gift since the beginning has been a very careful, detailed study of the subject and all its nuances, combining the Compass scenario play and parody. Rather than depending on the well-worn catchphrases and one or two ticks that plague so many parodies patterned after *Saturday Night Live* that build to a laugh and die within two minutes, the Free Associates take any piece— from Tennessee Williams plays to *ER* to *Dark Shadows*—and take the utmost care at copying everything possible, creating a very detailed list of suggestions to take from the audience.

Gagne, the group's artistic director for nearly ten years before finally hanging it up in early 2001, began in Boston, functioning there as the artistic director of the Boston ComedySportz for two and a half years before coming to Chicago and running the local franchise for another two and a half years. And despite the rewarding experience—Gagne cites ComedySportz founder Dick Chudnow as one of his greatest influences—he missed the rewarding experience of live theatre. Remember? The kind with real costumes and sets?

The first big hit for the Free Associates, who first held their shows in a small Wicker Park club called the Bop Shop, was *Pick-a-Dick,* an interactive, completely improvised parody of detective stories featuring some of our favorite literary sleuths, ranging from Mike Hammer to Nick and Nora Charles. Gagne states that he and his company sought out from the beginning to stay completely accurate to the source material, doing away with the improv tradition of object work in favor of a more theatrical setup.

For example, for their biggest hit, a parody of *ER* called *BS* (which stands for Benevolent Saints Hospital), the cast shows the audience what happened in the last episode, replaying three beats from the previous show to get them involved. And rather than simply asking for a single suggestion that has become the norm in long-form improvisation, the players announce to the audience members that *they* will be writing the next episode since NBC can't afford to pay its writing staff anymore. The cast asks them for very specific details around which the improvisers can create a new episode within the confines of the *ER* format.

Gagne is aware that some people insist that the idea of a scenario through which improvisers can work their magic is not true improvisation. He says, however, that setting up a structure like that can actually help an improviser. "I wanted to experiment with structured improv. I think an improviser can use the structure to free himself," he explains. Rather than seeing the structure as a limitation, Gagne believes that the improviser can use his or her creative abilities to the fullest when working within a discipline.

Rather than taking the mantle as improv, the Free Associates label much of their work as "unscripted parody." Much of what Chicago audiences, critics, and performers label as improv has been confined to thoughts of the Harold. The Free Associates' rendering of improvisation is different enough that using the term *improv* would suggest something far less theatrical and narrative based than what they were really presenting. Such is the bias of expectations.

Thus, their third unscripted parody and first big hit was *Cast on a Hot Tin Roof,* a dead-on parody of Tennessee Williams. Much of the Free Associates' work is defined by the intelligence of the parody choices. While something like *BS* parodies a television show, much of what the ensemble would attempt to create would be parodies of more obscure works, like their parody of the works of playwright Brian Friel, certainly not something you'll see on parody-based shows like *Saturday Night Live* or *Mad TV.*

In due part to the intelligence of their choices in their ten years, the Free Associates have often garnered favorable reviews. Still, Gagne and company do not rely entirely on their unscripted parodies. For example, one of the risks they took in recent years was an adaptation of the 1944 film noir classic *Laura* for the stage. No parody at all, the real thing. While this may have been unexpected, it is a further proof that Gagne loves theatre.

The Free Associates had a very successful run at the Ivanhoe Theater's second stage beginning in 1994 until the theatre was sold in January 2001. The space is now being used to expand an existing liquor store next door. Soon after the closing of the Ivanhoe, the show *BS* began an open run at the Royal George Theater. It wasn't until that August that a new show would appear in the Free Associate's repertoire, called *Alfred Hitchcock Resents.*

## The Playground

The origin of this latest theatre to enter Chicago's improv world can be directly attributed to the astounding success of ImprovOlympic's final move to a permanent stage in 1995. ImprovOlympic's new building, with two bars, two stages, and an entire staff of training center instructors, proved to be such an astounding success that the theatre could not have possibly accommodated the passions that burst forth from hundreds of students who walked through its doors to learn the Harold.

Within two years of opening the new facility, ImprovOlympic was in the enviable position of being in far too much demand. In order to facilitate the new talent that arrived, performers who had already trained there were forced off the performance stages. The problem was, dozens of these performers still wanted to improvise and did not have an easy platform from which they could expose their prodigious talents. Not every group would have the where-withal to produce their own shows at neighborhood bars like Halpern and Close did fifteen years previously. Thus, the idea of an improv co-op entered the mind of ImprovOlympic student and per-former Doug Diefenbach.

"We were founded to promote improv," says Doug Diefenbach, the Playground's founder. "This is a place created by and for impro-visers. In improv, you learn your craft and typically find that your performance opportunities are limited or that they're not in your control. We encourage artistic and marketing self-determination, along with a willingness to cooperate with other groups. Every-body's gotta be doing good work and take responsibility for what they're doing."

The concept was to bring together individual improvisational ensembles to form a theatre, the maintenance and continued sup-port of which they would share equally, from doing box office for shows to cleaning the theatre.

Artistically, each ensemble would be expected to present what-ever variation on improv it pleased. The focus was on long-form im-provisation, but the goal was to accept every style of improv that came along. In the four years hence, because of the theatre's roots in ImprovOlympic and the fact that so many hundreds of students study at ImprovOlympic, the vast majority of ensembles that have come along have performed long-form improvisation.

The founding nine ensembles congregated for the first time in April 1997. Ensembles ranged from Sheila, whose success in the '90s was unquestioned and whose participation lent an air of creditability to the venture, to new ensembles that were formed specifically for the co-op. Shows at first were uneven. However, as the theatre evolved, all level of improvisers who no longer took classes at ImprovOlympic and other training centers like Second City were able to find a refuge at the Playground and the quality of shows improved.

Saddled with having to perform in noisy bars for nearly two years, the Playground finally found a home. Opening in March 1999, the Playground Theater began to experience a radical improvement in its shows, which—following in the footsteps of ImprovOlympic—featured four improv groups, each performing whatever form it wished for twenty-five minutes. The vast majority of improv groups did long form and would do just about any form covered in this book and far more outside the confines of this book. Says Diefenbach, "We have the widest range of improv styles you can see on any one stage. We give improvisers the freedom and direction. They don't have to fit into a specific improv box."

As performers became accustomed to not having to shout in order to be heard over the din of bar patrons, their styles became more suited to the intimate sixty-seat venue. Slower scenes and an overall emphasis on characterization and honest interaction became the theme at the theatre. Many performers began studying a more legitimate acting style at local training center the Artistic Home, where the teachings of Sanford Meisner were taught. Further study of how Meisner is used in long-form improv appears in a later chapter.

As the first nonprofit improv co-op theatre in the country, the Playground also features RECESS (Really Excellent Classroom Enhancement Through Silliness and Satire), an outreach program that emphasizes Viola Spolin's vision of improv games as a children's training exercise. The theatre sends three or four of its improvisers to local schools and various children's organizations around Chicago, focusing often on children who come from a disadvantaged economic background or children with developmental disabilities, places like Children's Memorial Hospital and the Boys and Girls Clubs. The improvisers not only perform but teach the children basic improv games, truly becoming an extension of the earliest improvisational workshops in the first half of the last century.

The Playground Theater also produces shows as part of what it calls the Director's Series. They invite a prominent improvisational director to create a long form with a cast consisting mostly of performers from the Playground's various member ensembles. The first Director's Series production, called *Dinner for Six,* a revival of a show that had an original run at ImprovOlympic, was conceived and directed by Jason Chin. The show followed the romantic relationships of three couples in one of the more successful recent attempts to create a fully improvised one-act play. The show was a hit with critics and audiences and was soon followed by *Drive,* a long form directed by Meisner-style director Rob Mello, and additional shows directed by Chicago directors like Peter Gwinn, Andy Eninger, and Dan Izzo.

According to Diefenbach, the Playground pursues improv as a mission, not a business. The overriding philosophy is that improv goes beyond mere entertainment: "Improv demonstrates how teamwork, trust, and support can make something wonderful out of absolutely nothing.

"We're a place for people who are really committed to improv," continues Diefenbach, "for those who have gotten past that first blush of being on stage. Improvisers need to know that they can make the Playground their theatre, and they will be embraced. We want people to come here and take over the place. The artistic freedom we provide encourages people to experiment within a supportive environment. . . . That experimentation and acceptance means that in one night on our stage, audiences get to see the widest possible range of improv styles in Chicago, many of them highly innovative."

Besides the member ensembles on the Playground Theater's stage, in order to foster the idea of variety, existing ensembles throughout the Chicago area are invited to become guest ensembles, performing once every month or two. As Diefenbach explains, "We member groups do the work to keep this stage open as a place where the outsider can come and experiment, gain stage time, play with new people, etc."

Other programs the Playground fosters are the Master's Series, a series of "advanced workshops for working improvisers" intended to improve specific skills in improvisers who have already gone through the training centers at Second City, ImprovOlympic, or the Annoyance. They also have their Incubator program. Performers who are not currently in an ensemble audition for this program, as well as performers who may already be in an ensemble but merely want a chance to play with some new people. Groups are formed and rehearse for a couple of months before performing in two special midweek shows where they can perform in the ease of an environment consisting of fellow Incubator ensembles and invite friends and family to shows. Then, once they have "graduated" after another few months performing in Thursday shows, the Incubator ensembles are "let go" and given independence to do what they like with their group, whether it's continue to perform at the Playground or elsewhere.

In less than five years the Playground has gone from nothing to one of the better places to perform and see improv in Chicago.

## WNEP Theater (Originally Level 6)

Spawned from the Second City Training Center, WNEP Theater found its life in early 1993. Classmates Don Hall, Joe Janes, and Jeff Hoover saw a show called *Cannibal Cheerleaders on Crack,* put up by a company called Torso Theater, and decided "if they can put up that kind of crap, we can do much better," according to Hall.

At the Second City Training Center, the program ends with Level Five, so this company of what Don Hall called "a former stand-up comedian, a middle school teacher, an impressionist, and seven others who had all gone through the Second City Training Center together" called themselves Level 6. After about eighteen months, the ensemble decided they had had enough of attempting Second City–style sketch comedy revues and decided to go for collaboratively written, original plays.

The company also changed their name from Level 6 to WNEP Theater, WNEP standing for What Now Entertainment Productions. The first play, a great success, was *The Armageddon Radio Hour,* a darkly comic look at a radio special that is broadcast one hour before the end of the world. The content of the show would change weekly, with new material brought in by the whole cast. "The thing I like about the initial group is everybody's ideas are given equal weight," says Hall.

While WNEP members write plays collaboratively, they haven't forgotten improvisation. Not all of their shows are improvised and

Hall believes that if they choose to do an improv show "artistically, if we use improvisation, it *has* to be improvised." Something, for example, like *Post Mortem,* says Hall. The completely improvised show takes obituary notices of people and improvises something along the lines of "A Day in the Life." In a show like that, the improvisation itself is the basis for the show, says Hall, and the content and concept of the show does not lend itself to something that is scripted. The immediacy of the obituary notices is central to the show. Another unique part of this show is that it is not intended to be completely comic.

According to WNEP's current artistic director, Jen Ellison, "The first WNEP show I saw was *Metaluna* and I found it to be unlike anything else in town. Not only was it very intelligent, it was subversive and entertaining."

Ellison created an Artistic Steering Committee composed of herself and four company members and began the process of transforming an improv-based, comedic theatre group into a theatre with a truly dark, eccentric voice. Under her guidance, *Grotesque Lovesongs, The Mysteries of Harris Burdick, . . . apocalypse . . . ,* and *Wise Blood* came to fruition.

"We still utilize improvisation," notes Black Box Series director Seth Fisher. "It has become one of the many theatrical tools we use rather than the meat and potatoes of WNEP." Besides an ensemble-based improvisational show like *Post Mortem,* one of the theatre's best-received improvisational shows was the two-person *My Grandma's a Fat Whore in New Jersey.* The success of this show prompted many more duos to put up long-form improvisational forms.

In the year 2000, WNEP Theater took its place in its first permanent home. Original plays take up the prime-time Thursday through Sunday slots, while other shows like *Post Mortem* enjoy open-ended runs in the off-night and late-night slots.

WNEP enjoys sort of a rough-and-tumble reputation that the Annoyance Theater had in its heyday. If one were forced to define WNEP's whole artistic philosophy, Hall says it would best be described as "Dadaist surrealist." The popularity of this theatre is increasing all the time, with new ensemble members coming aboard constantly. They've even started teaching their own improv classes, more oriented like the Playground's Master's Series, with teachers

Rob Mello and Monica Payne teaching Meisner and improv in single-day workshops.

## The Noble Fool Theater

Current Noble Fool player and director Jack Bronis first became involved with improvisational theatre when he met John Michelski, who was part of Improv Institute, which Bronis soon joined. The Improv Institute had a theatre on the North Side from 1984 until 1994, where they mostly did game-based improvisation. The theatre was moderately successful and then came up with a big hit in *Flanagan's Wake.*

*Flanagan's Wake,* as the title would suggest, is an Irish wake, offering an interactive environment in which the audience can participate. Much of the show is scripted, the beats written out like a Compass scenario play; however, much of the show itself is improvised. Bronis created the show, and it became such a hit that Bronis and company felt they had to separate the show from the Improv Institute. Soon afterward, Zeitgeist Theater emerged. In 1994, the Institute on West Belmont closed, leaving only Zeitgeist Theater performing *Flanagan's Wake* every week.

The show was joined in 1999 by a *Sopranos* parody, called *The Baritones.* Shows were performed at places like the Royal George Theater while Zeitgeist looked for a permanent home, during which time they decided to change their name again once they realized not everyone knew what *Zeitgeist* meant. After another long, laborious process, they chose the Noble Fool, which was a line from Shakespeare's *As You Like It.*

Then, something rather amazing and unexpected happened: The city of Chicago decided to revive its Loop Theater District, an area that had been moribund for decades, the only surviving active facility in the early 1990s being the Chicago Theater, which had been traded from owner to owner.

Other theatres in the area directly surrounding Randolph Street in the Loop had long gone into disrepair. The city decided to renovate theatres like the Oriental Theater and the Palace, which would become the Ford Center for the Performing Arts and the Cadillac Palace, respectively. The legendary Goodman Theater would build a brand-new facility, and a brand-new home for the Film Center for the School of the Arts Institute would be built as the Gene Siskel Film Center.

The next bombshell was that the city of Chicago decided to help the Noble Fool come downtown. It gave $1 million in TIF (tax increment financing) assistance to the company to help subsidize its $2.5 million complex.

The bilevel 8,000-square-foot facility will include three performance spaces: a mainstage of 155 seats, a 100-seat studio, and a comedy and music cabaret. The original facade of the building—a Bavarian baroque design for the Old Heidelberg Restaurant—is fully restored. The building is nestled in between the Oriental Theater and a bookstore off of the revitalized State Street.

The 100-seat studio will feature the newly transplanted *Flanagan's Wake,* and the cabaret will feature improvisation from the Noble Fool members as well as other improv ensembles from throughout the city. The mainstage will have a traditional theatre season like we see at establishments like the Goodman and Steppenwolf.

To illustrate what will appear at the mainstage, according to their website the inaugural season will open with *The Viking Show.* It "takes the audience back a millennium to the Golden Age of the feared and fearless men from the North. Join Olaf and his cheery band of Viking warriors as they wreak havoc upon society, and attempt to teach the proper way to disembowel one's enemies (With special appearances by Thor and Odin)." It's an original work, but the theatre also features a revival of *Lovers and Other Strangers* by Joe Bologna and Renee Taylor, so the comedic content will indeed vary.

As the first theatre to feature improvisation and improvisationally based material downtown, it may be an interesting peek at the possibilities of other theatres to take a stab at the Loop.

## GayCo Productions

GayCo Productions is a literal child of Second City. Second City had its African American outreach in 1996 and Ed Garza, who was a performer who also ran the training center at the time, pushed for a gay and lesbian outreach. Second City owner Andrew Alexander supported the idea and there were workshops in September and October of 1996, bringing in nine people from various classes, working with different people.

Then, Second City gave them the great gift of Jeff Richmond. Richmond, who had been the piano accompanist for shows at the Second City e.t.c. as well as the Level Five shows at the Second City Training Center, would be the full director of this, his first revue under the Second City banner. The show was put together with gay and lesbian themes in mind. However, besides that, they followed the format of Second City shows by rehearsing improvisational scenes and then building written sketches out of them.

Their first revue was ready to open in early 1997, called *Whitney Houston, We Have a Problem*. However, there was a problem. Donny's Skybox Theater, named after director and teacher Don DePollo, who had passed away recently, was having problems opening. Entertainment license problems were delaying the opening of the show and the cast had to be on call from one weekend to the next awaiting resolution to their problem.

GayCo founding member Andy Eninger remembers, "We were on continuous tech for four weeks, rehearsing two or three times a week, thinking that 'this might be the weekend we open!'"

"By the time we opened, we were incredibly polished," to which Eninger attributes the success of the show both financially and critically. A first run was an astounding success and they remounted the production later that year.

After the second run, Second City producer Kelly Leonard said to them that "Second City can't support you the way we did the first show, but we want to see you succeed, so here's the same crew including Jeff Richmond. Do your own thing."

After the second show opened, GayCo was invited to Amsterdam for the Gay Games and in order to go through the fund-raising necessary for such a venture, GayCo had to incorporate as a nonprofit organization and then go through the necessary routines to raise money to go overseas.

In looking at GayCo and its continuing success as an independent nonprofit organization, Eninger relates, "Increasingly, the five founding members who remain set an artistic idea for a show and deliver that to the director. In this case, *When Bush Comes to Shove*, the spring 2001 show, we wanted to the show to be more physical, more of a circus atmosphere, and gave that agenda to Martin Garcia, the show's director. Before, the director would select the scenes based on their own whims."

In the past two years, GayCo Productions has incorporated into a nonprofit organization and put together a board of directors. Andrew Alexander expresses interest in joining the board and while GayCo is not under the auspices of Second City anymore, Second City still contributes its expertise in organization development to the fledgling organization. As Eninger puts it, "They're very committed to see that we don't die."

GayCo is a sigh of relief in the improv community in Chicago, which for years has been aggressively male and heterosexual.

## Chicago Comedy Company

Chicago Comedy Company began as a group called Katabasis, but, according to cofounder Andy Eninger, "we really missed the improv but wanted to bring the professionalism to improv, something from which we could make a living.

"We shed our skin like a cicada and became the Chicago Comedy Company in '97, just started off just to do improv. Steve Matuszak was a big driving force; we quickly realized that a little professionalism went a long way and sent our product to colleges."

The company was a success, getting plenty of gigs playing standard improv games at colleges and community centers while flexing its long-form improvisation muscles as a member ensemble of the Playground Theatre. Still, there were greater professional opportunities in the corporate sector, something that the Second City had taken advantage of for years with their Business Theatre. The concept is to create customized shows for corporations, usually at all-employee gatherings.

Eninger explains, "Usually a gig will look like this: They call us. They say, 'We called Second City. Are you cheaper?' We'll say, 'Probably.' We'll figure out what they're looking for—it's usually something like an employee recognition dinner where they want to bring in some comedy and moderately customized—give them a proposal and price . . . and it's always less than Second City."

When they get the gig, Eninger says, "We interview the contact person, interview two to ten people at the company, get to know what's it like, get into the world. At a place like Kaplan, we might show a scene of what it's like for a central manager to get people to take a GRE Prep Test." Then, after the research, they present the scenes and games with an ensemble of anywhere from three to five people.

"We've built ourselves up by word of mouth and the Internet has been huge. The Internet is the great equalizer. People look for this sort of product and find Second City first and then us."

The corporate work that Chicago Comedy Company has gotten has made making it into the ensemble one of the few methods by which a person can get paid for performing improvisational comedy.

Of course, there are countless improvisers who may some day get the chance to create their own theatres. Often, when another springs up, there are those who say that the market cannot support another theatre. Even more often, they're wrong. The audience for improv keeps growing and if a group of people can put an interesting enough twist on the form, they can thrive in the current environment.

Following the lead of ImprovOlympic, many improvisers attempt to put that twist on the theatre. When it comes to making the artistic choices, there are many more ways an improviser can express himself or herself.

# Building on the Harold

In touching on the Harold in Chapter 3, one sees that there are many ways upon which improvisers can build on the basic concepts established in that structure. One of the reasons the Harold is so brilliant is its inherent simplicity. Building the basic structure of themes, patterns, and the Time Dash allows improvisers the freedom to explore the potential of improv, limited only by their own willingness to be fully accepting of what their fellow players explore.

The long-form improvisation style that the Harold embraces allows improvisers to build their own structure around which themes and patterns can emerge. While studying the Harold at Improv-Olympic for nearly two decades, students, performers, and directors have often gone on to discover their own long forms and interpretations of what constitutes improvisation.

Since the Harold, as created by Del Close in the late 1960s, is a long form that simply encourages themes and patterns rather than something with a formal structure, there are those who believe that all long forms following this concept are simply the Harold with a different coat of paint.

For example, a long-form ensemble may decide that they want to create a new form. The form begins with an opening where they carry a telephone book on stage with them. They ask the audience for a page number in the telephone book, at which point a player opens to that page, closes her eyes, and points to a random point on the page. Opening her eyes, she reads the listing to which she pointed. That listing then functions as the suggestion and a long form ensues, with an opening that riffs off the telephone listing and then a series of scenes building themes and patterns through the piece.

The only difference between this scenario and what some people believe is a true Harold is the use of the telephone book. Is this a particularly new or unique form or simply another little thing to add to the audience's feeling that they—through their suggestion—really drive what is going on on stage?

Regardless of whether one thinks a different method of getting the audience suggestion is another form, the recurring pattern in the last fifteen years is that improvisers in Chicago desire ownership of the work they do on stage. Since improvisation is often a very personal discovery, improvisers feel if they invent a form rather than repeating what has been done before, it is somehow worthier. It is one of the reasons many new improv theatres spring up so often. A sense of ownership and feeling like you're doing something new are important.

This pursuit of ownership has stimulated numerous productions in Chicago, whether they are at an established institution like ImprovOlympic or in a basement theatre where you can rent the space for thirty-five dollars a night.

So many variations on long form have been created in the last fifteen years that it's impossible to put them all down in this one volume, unless one wants to carry around a fifty-pound improv book. Del Close himself created dozens of forms at ImprovOlympic, first as exercises in class and then for performances. He created variations on the Harold itself in a show called *Night of the Mutant Harolds* in 1995, utilizing the house team Missing Fersons. They performed three variations on the Harold. The first was Monologue Harold, in which scenes were created improvisationally through monologues. No direct interaction between characters occurred, even when there were more than one person in a certain location. It's as if scenes are composed entirely of asides. The Dream Harold did not receive a suggestion from the audience at all, the opening scene consisting of one player describing a dream she recently had.

The Solo Harold was one player performing a Harold with multiple characters all by himself or herself, something that was later adapted unknowingly by Andy Eninger, who developed a form called Sybil.

Late in his life, Close taught a performance class at ImprovOlympic (also known as Level Five B) in which students who completed the last level of classes there would create their own form and perform it for a limited run in the Del Close Theater. One form was called Slam Dunk, in which improvisations came from poetry the players themselves created and then performed in a poetry slam–type opening. Another was Questionable Characters, which consisted of interviews of a single player as an opening.

At ImprovOlympic, one of the more popular shows that emerged on Monday nights as a way for busy alumni to continue improvising when they didn't have to work at Second City was the Armando Diaz Theatrical Experience and Hootenanny, a form that gained much popularity. The improviser and teacher Armando Diaz would get a suggestion and begin a long storytelling-style monologue from which the inspired players would improvise scenes, edited sometimes by Diaz, who would continue his long monologue throughout the two-act show. Once Diaz himself stopped doing the shows, different improvisers would take turns being Armando Diaz. After a couple of years, new improvisers did not realize that Armando Diaz was, in fact, a real person.

Following Close, when one looks at different improvisational long forms, one should see an interesting twist at how the ensemble arrives at themes and patterns, both conceptual and narrative. Simply changing the method of obtaining the audience suggestion or changing the opening of the Harold isn't really enough to say that it's different from the Harold. Many improvisers—Close included—attempted to put new spins on the idea of long-form improvisation and following are some examples of Close's and his followers' attempts to expand the ideas of improvisation even more.

## Deconstruction

Kevin Mullaney is a teacher at the Upright Citizens Brigade Theater in New York City. The UCB Theater, as it is usually known, was begun by four protégés of Close and Halpern who formed the Upright

Citizens Brigade, which created gloriously antisocial sketch comedy and spent three seasons on television on Comedy Central. Moving to New York in the mid-'90s, the UCB began teaching the Harold themselves, finally opening their own theatre in 1998. Since then, the long-form improvisational movement in NYC has flowered. Their training center actually has more students than the training center at ImprovOlympic in Chicago.

Kevin Mullaney himself joined the faculty in early 1999, after spending years performing, teaching, and directing at the Improv-Olympic. He was a member of the IO house team Frank Booth, a group that spawned some of the top long-form improv teachers and directors in the country, including Lillie Frances, Paul Grondy, and Liz Allen, who now runs the training center at IO.

According to Mullaney, one can say that all long forms in the ImprovOlympic school of thought are actually deconstructions of the single suggestion made at the top of the show. However, one form was specifically labeled as the Deconstruction. The Deconstruction was popularized at IO during the show *Three Mad Rituals* in 1993.

Mullaney remembers, "The Deconstruction as it was taught to me was a specific form. The version of it that we did at Improv-Olympic was a form that started with a long two-person scene that acted as the opening for the rest of the piece so that everything that happened after that first scene somehow drew on a piece of the first scene."

Doing such a scene that would inhabit all the scenes that followed would require breaking a few of the general notions of scenes in a Harold. Mullaney pointed out the difference. "For instance, the first scene generally should be a longer, slower-paced [one] than you would do normally, more conversational probably than you would do normally. It should be more varied than you would do normally," he explained. "Normally at IO and here at UCB, we try to get people to get very focused with their scenework so it has one game. Everything serves that game in that scene and in the first scene in a Deconstruction, if you do that, then you're going to have very limited information to deal with. So it's better to have a conversational scene where it can wander; it should go into new territory, it should have non sequiturs, so that you can get a lot of different territory out of it."

This is a direct violation of one of the simplest and most sacred of improv rules: to avoid storytelling. For example, in the first scene of a Deconstruction, Bob and Dan are mowing the lawn. In the context of a Harold or other long form, the coach or director would want the two scene partners to use their environment but stay in the moment, concentrating on the relationship and game in that moment. The game might involve Dan being a poorer mower than Bob and that somehow would ignite the game in the scene.

If this scene were the first scene in a Deconstruction, perhaps we would see Dan relate *why* he is such a bad mower. Here is where storytelling is a must. Dan can fill his story with details. He became a bad mower because his father was in the Cuban revolution in 1959, smoked cigars with Fidel Castro, and only called to tell little Danny boy to mow the lawn and Dan *in fact* is an excellent mower but just does it badly to spite his Communist father. During the course of the story, Dan can make references to cereal; flag burning; Emerson, Lake, and Palmer; Ed Sullivan; shoeshine boys in Union Station; duck hunting; and the names of the first three women with whom he had intercourse.

A scene like this is extraordinarily unwise and would be severely reprimanded in the normal context of an improv workshop. A player must remember, however, that after that first scene, things return to normal and the conversational anti-scene should be thrown to the wayside. Mullaney continues, "After that point, it's mostly scenes, although like the Harold you can do things that more resemble group games or you could do monologues or whatever.

"But mostly it's scenes after the initial scene and those scenes connect to the original scene in one of a few different ways," Mullaney adds.

"For instance, you could bring back characters from the actual scenes, so you take one of those characters and see them in a new location. You probably explore something they may have mentioned offhand. Let's say one of the characters mentioned that they were going duck hunting. You might see a scene with him and some other guys duck hunting, so that would be a fairly direct way you take one of the characters and put them in a different place."

Mullaney says, "More broadly, you could do things that sort of generally fit in those surroundings. Let's say the original scene takes place in an office building. Then you might see other people who work in the same company. Very obviously people working in the same company are connected with those people's lives but those characters don't *have* to show up. Often you might have a character mentioned in the first scene; you know, somebody's mom or uncle or something, and that becomes the basis. We see that uncle or that mother or ex-girlfriend or whatever in a later scene, again with or without the characters that actually showed up in the first scene.

"And then I guess there would be scenes that are based on just information from the scene. It could be they talk about shoes for a little while so we see a scene in a shoestore but these characters have nothing to do directly with the original scene. Or there's an *idea*. I always found it was helpful to have characters who spouted points of view in the opening scene, you know? 'The world would be better without all these damn vegetarians' and move on. And then maybe later you see a scene where you know it poses that question: What would the world be like without vegetarians? How much better would the world be without vegetarians?"

In performing improvisational theatre, Mullaney points out that the performers, as immersed as they are in improvising their scenes well, cannot forget the audience and their perception of the work. The audience needs to have the opportunity to understand the form. Mullaney believes that a form needs to be designed for the audience member who doesn't know anything about it beforehand. He says for example, "If you do three scenes in a row that use characters from the first scene and then suddenly do a scene with nothing involved—no direct connection with the first scene—then the audience gets confused and the audience tries to figure out . . . they ask, 'What does this have to do with this? I don't get it.'"

His suggestion is to somehow establish in the first couple of scenes that not all scenes have to be directly connected to the opening scene. He explains, "The ones that don't go off a direct connection, the ones that go off an idea or a word from the opening scene, we refer to as tangent scenes, and if you have a tangent scene right off the bat then it gets the audience used to those kinds of things. They say 'Oh, other things can happen!'"

Mullaney adds that interestingly enough, Del Close—at the beginning of teaching this form—thought the term *deconstruction* was an incorrect label for the form. The accepted definition of the term *deconstruction* is:

> A philosophical movement and theory of literary criticism that questions traditional assumptions about certainty, identity, and truth, asserts that words can only refer to other words, and attempts to demonstrate how statements about any text subvert their own meanings: "In deconstruction, the critic claims there is no meaning to be found in the actual text, but only in the various, often mutually irreconcilable, 'virtual texts' constructed by readers in their search for meaning."

The idea that taking a primary scene and peeling away the layers of it was deconstruction did not sit well with Close but, as Mullaney relates, "I think over time he started to think that was actually a good name for it. Actually, that *was* actually kind of what was happening, especially in the tangent scenes with the ideas when someone would put forth an idea or would say something that implies that they have a belief structure, or that actually deconstruction *was* happening. You were taking an idea that maybe seemed to be an assumption of the scene and seeing that assumption played out somewhere else and that's kind of the process of deconstruction as I understand it."

Mullaney continued, "So it was really related and that actually had a huge effect and what you had after that point [was] you had lots and lots of forms that deconstructed things, that deconstructed monologues, that was probably the most used, like the *Armando Diaz* show in Chicago and *ASSSCAT* in New York, are monologue deconstructions and probably another dozens of shows, especially in Chicago where you're working off monologues primarily, but other things have been tried as well, deconstructed poems and songs, and basically, newspaper articles. Basically anything could be deconstructed.

"Some people say Deconstruction is a form of the Harold, but you could argue the other, that the deconstruction is a more general form. Depending on how you define the Harold, the Harold is a deconstruction.

"The original idea of the Deconstruction was that everything goes back to the beginning. Whenever you start a new scene, it's always brand new; it has something to do with the beginning, but it's always brand new. As opposed to the Harold, where you do second and third beats where they are a continuation in some sense to the first beats."

## La Ronde

A rehearsal exercise that eventually saw itself evolve into a full-fledged form in performance was La Ronde. The name La Ronde comes from a play by Arthur Schnitzler, who is best known today as the author of the novel *Traumnovelle,* which served as the basis for the film *Eyes Wide Shut.* In 1950, French filmmaker Max Ophuls made his version of *La Ronde,* a carousel of the sexual exploits of the aristocracy. One character enters the scene and beds another. Then that character moves on and beds another until the whole thing wraps up with the final character introduced, bedding the first character from the first scene.

Not quite so provocatively interpreted in the context of impro-visational theatre, La Ronde became a perfect character study for improv groups in Chicago who studied at ImprovOlympic. Mullaney explains, "La Ronde started popping up around the same time as the Deconstruction, as a sort of a game that Del would play in class, and other people picked up on it. I think a lot of groups would do it in rehearsal and not know what else to do with it. In Frank Booth, we did loads and loads of La Rondes in rehearsal; we never did one on stage."

In adapting the form, the exercise is, as Mullaney puts it, "a se-ries of scenes where you have the first scene between two charac-ters. The second scene takes one of the characters and replaces him or her with a new character." Thus, Character A and B do a scene together, Character A exits and we see Character B play with Char-acter C. B exits, and D enters to play with Character C, until it all circles around. Character D then exits, to be replaced by Character A. This follows the format of the film, except—unlike the film—the subject is not necessarily the pursuit of love and/or sex. We see two different facets of each character."

Mullaney continues, "I don't really remember what Del was us-ing it for, but I remember what I liked about it and what I always used it for. A lot of people do 'tagouts.'" A tagout is when two peo-ple might be in a scene and another player comes into the scene and tags one player out of the scene. The new person will then take the position of the tagged-out player as that player exits the stage and then start a brand-new scene. Mullaney says the player who does the tagout will often do it when she realizes she can play the same scenic game in a new situation.

"Tagouts tend to speed things up," Mullaney says. "They tend to really exploit the game and so forth, and sometimes people do a La Ronde and use it to do *that,* to hit the game from character to character. But what I've always liked to do is really, in a way, do the opposite of that, where we see two characters and we tag in a character and we ask a new question of that character.

"Let's say we have two cops on a stakeout talking about some bust that they did a few nights before and they're talking about their job and whatever; so we have this scene and it explores these two characters. What you could do is tag a character out and then you see one of these cops in an interrogation room interrogating a suspect or we see him talking to the chief of police and it's more police stuff about this character. I've always encouraged people to instead tag that out and find something *new* about this character. If, for instance, the police characters haven't talked about their family then let's *see* them with their family. Let's see them deal with their wife or their son or daughter or their mother. Let's see them—if we haven't talked about what they do for fun—let's see them with their rock-climbing club. Let's see them in a different sphere of their lives. Of course the characters are going to have similarities and you want them to bring those similarities forward, but it becomes a much more creative kind of thing.

"It encourages people to explore their characters and that's what we did when we did it with Frank Booth. That's what it encouraged us to do and helped us with the second beats in our Harolds to make them more explorative so it wasn't just that we were taking these characters and bringing them to a second beat and nailing the game again, but we were asking new questions often of our characters in our second beats and that's when it was most pleasurable.

"Finding a way to play a new game that fits with these characters rather than just mechanically going about playing the same game."

In January 1997, Kevin Mullaney was dispatched—while still in Chicago—to direct a show with Cinco de Bob, an improv group that had completed its run as a Harold team at ImprovOlympic five months beforehand. The show was to take place at the O Bar, a small jazz martini bar in Chicago, in the thirty-seat basement theatre. Mullaney and another member of Frank Booth, Lillie Frances, had introduced La Ronde to the ensemble during rehearsals for ImprovOlympic the previous summer.

The goal was to create a performance piece out of the rehearsal tool. Mullaney says, "The form was probably the first I can remember of someone directly doing La Ronde."

Consisting of traditional two- or three-minute scenes with an eight-member cast, the La Ronde rehearsal exercise would inevitably end in less than half an hour, not nearly the amount of time necessary to present a show that one could advertise as a production and charge potential audiences for it.

"It couldn't be a whole form in itself," says Mullaney, "and it always kind of felt to me like a beginning, like it was a way to set something up. So that's what we started working on, this idea that we're going to use a La Ronde to set up a community of characters and then when the La Ronde was complete we would see a lot of other scenes.

"In a sense, we would be deconstructing La Ronde, which would be a very large opening, where we set up all these characters and then we come back and continue to do those kinds of moves." For example, the Character A referred to earlier will end up doing a scene with Character C and then Character C may do a scene with Character E, and so on.

"That was the whole thing. The thing that I liked best about it was this sense of community," Mullaney explains. "The way we were encouraged to do the Harold was that these characters did not have an original connection. When you start out the first three scenes of a Harold, you want them to be as disparate as possible and [with] La Ronde and some other things I worked on, the idea was these characters should be different from one another. They shouldn't be like, you know, eight cops that all seem to act the same, but of having a community. You know, maybe it's the police, their wives, and some other people that are connected in the same sort of community, like the paramedics or something, you know. So you have a fairly broad mix of things but there is a connecting fiber between these characters and we know pretty soon after we start what this connecting fiber is so this is gonna be this form about, you know, tonight it's going to be about this hospital or this camp or this school or something."

## Close Quarters

Another form that concentrated on community, but in a much more unique fashion, was the one introduced in the show *Close Quarters*. ImprovOlympic and Second City National Touring Company veteran Peter Gwinn put together an "all-star" cast of performers and hired Noah Gregoropoulos as director.

Gregoropoulos was a member of Jazz Freddy and had become a well-regarded director. He remembers, "As a result of the attention of Jazz Freddy, as usually happens, Kelly [Leonard] hired half the cast of Jazz Freddy soon thereafter." The cast eventually became part of the cast of *Lois Kaz*.

"All of a sudden you had all these great long-form improvisers . . . some of them he already had, he just didn't know he had, or didn't know what they could do outside of the single-scene format."

Soon, various improvisers who worked for Second City's touring company began to get the itch to try a long-form show at Second City. Gregoropoulos remembers, "They were basically Dave Koechener and Kevin Dorff, who were sort of clamoring in his ear, 'Y'know, why don't you hire Noah and we'll do a long-form show here? Because no one's ever done one at Second City, you got all these great people.' They were all in various touring companies, which can be a lot of fun, but it can also be sort of artistically stifling to be in one."

So Kelly Leonard decided to go for it and hired Noah Gregoropoulos to direct the show that would be known as *Lois Kaz,* named after a longtime employee of the Second City administrative offices. Gregoropoulos says, "So we got together a pretty outstanding cast . . . and to Kelly's credit, he didn't let me just take all the people from Jazz Freddy. When he approached me about it, he said, 'Who do you want to use?' I said, 'Well, all the people from Jazz Freddy!'

"He's like, 'Well, politically, I can't let you do that.' So that forced us to look seriously at the other people he had, which expanded the cast to a good spread of people. And there was nothing particularly earth shattering about the show itself. It was fairly straightforward, not a challenging form; I think it was more impor- tant that it put long form on the map at Second City."

The show was a huge success, running Tuesday nights, which was an off-night at the Second City e.t.c. Kelly Leonard was a huge fan and the show, in many ways, led to *Piñata Full of Bees*.

After the success of *Lois Kaz*, Gregoropoulos' next show at Sec- ond City e.t.c. had one of the more challenging forms ever per- formed in Chicago.

A cast member of *Close Quarters*, Craig Cackowski, is currently a teacher at ImprovOlympic in Chicago. He was in *Close Quarters* along with Gwinn, Lillie Frances, Al Samuels, Molly Cavanaugh, Rich Talarico, Stephnie Weir, and Bob Dassie. He recalls that the re- hearsal process for the show was quite extensive, at least by the standards of completely improvised productions. Most improvisa- tional ensembles or shows will often rehearse once a week for a couple of months. The cast of *Close Quarters* rehearsed for about four or five months, three times a week. In a community that is sometimes criticized for lack of commitment and effort, this was re- markable, especially considering that many of the performers were constantly touring with Second City.

Cackowski recalls, "The first rehearsal was very memorable. It was in Stephnie Weir's backyard. It must have been early fall, the last nice day in the fall. We just played in the backyard. It was a Sat- urday or Sunday afternoon. We just did some scenes and we worked on heightening characters as opposed to following the plot of the scene. We would do 'character dashes,' and Noah would get on us if we were . . . let's say the character is a doctor. If the fact that he was a doctor was influencing our choices rather than the way this person *behaved,* then Noah would get on us.

"Doctor is just one detail of this person's life. Instead, we should be working on heightening his arrogance or his naïveté or his sensitivity or whatever, some other aspect of his personality. We could go into the past, we could go into the future, so that charac- ter dash that we worked on in that first day of rehearsal was kind of a staple of the form from then on. And to this day, there are memorable scenes from that first rehearsal that Talarico still talks about, something where we were the two least popular kids in a marching band camp and I turned on him and said, 'Go play your tuba, Fatty.' It was a fat kid that even me, the most pathetic kid, picked on."

Director Noah Gregoropoulos remembers that first rehearsal as well. "I literally could walk you around town this past weekend to every improv show in town and you couldn't see better improv than we had in the backyard of Steph's apartment building."

These character dashes ended up contributing to the developing form. Cackowski believes Gregoropoulos had this form in mind before rehearsals began and just needed some guinea pigs upon which to work. Gregoropoulos attributes his idea to the Jim Jarmusch film *Mystery Train*.

Says Cackowski, "The form was comprised of heightening characters. That was kind of the scenework aspect of it, and the other aspect of it was that we were covering a very short period of time in a very small area of space. So over an hour-long form, we might just be in a bowling alley but we would shift from location to location throughout the bowling alley: different lanes, the bathroom, behind the counter, outside where teenagers are hanging out . . . many different sublocations within this one general location but in a very tight area where the characters might wander in and out of other people's spaces and the time aspect, we hoped to cover the same fifteen minutes over and over in an hour.

"So, the first scene of the night might be the last scene chronologically. We hoped to link up scenes chronologically by hearing voices offstage that would be in an adjacent space and then we would use those lines to link up scenes in time." Using the bowling alley example, we may see a scene at the bar between a boyfriend and girlfriend where the girlfriend is yelling at him, something like, "You never loved me!" Later in the form, we may see a scene between a couple at the water fountain next to the bar and hear the girlfriend's exclamation again, offstage. This method was used to overlap scenes and make the audience aware that the performers were covering fifteen minutes of chronology in an hour-long performance.

Cackowski says, laughing, "Although, you know, at the end of the show, we tried to do a tight chronology of the fifteen minutes, you know, and found it couldn't possibly have worked out, things would not make sense, but generally we were covering a very short period of time."

Regarding the structure of the piece, Gregoropoulos says, "It was a goal. I didn't care if it was fifteen minutes or an hour and a half. Normally in improv you start at a point and flower outward. I was asking them to cross back through the same point over and over and over again so that would resonate. And that you couldn't tell much of a story because it wasn't going to last very long. It couldn't last much longer than a scene lasts, in terms of narrative time, and what that causes is you continue to widen the iris on a single moment rather than follow a path, and to me that heightens the scenic side of improv because of the focus on the moment in improv. It's really the only form where narrative is really de-emphasized. And having worked briefly in Hollywood, it's so refreshing to be denied thinking about the story. All that anyone thinks about when they make the movie, they just think about the story and leave out everything else. I love a good story, it's part of man's artistic definition, but it's not all of art. There are paintings and improv, too."

In explaining the character dash concentration of the form, Cackowski says, "Each scene would start out as a two-person scene and build up into a cast scene but with one character being heightened in each scene. So if the first scene was me and you and then Rich wanted to heighten your character, he would come in and engage you. I would still be in the scene with you but now you're doing two different two-person scenes then. Steph would come in and engage you—another character from your life, another aspect of your personality. [They are] the kind of choices you would make if you were doing a series of tagouts. 'Okay, well this is this guy with his boss. Let's see what he's like with his girlfriend. Let's see what he's like with his doctor. Let's see what he's like with his next-door neighbor.' Except we're doing it all in the same time and space. The other characters would never talk to the people they weren't engaged with. So if I'm your boss and then Rich comes in as your brother, he never talks to me as the boss. Everything is through you. He knows I'm there, he might even mention that I'm there, but all the dialogue flows through *you*."

By concentrating on engaging a single character, "it also freed us to not make choices that were dictated by the space, so if you're in a doctor's office it doesn't have to be all doctors and nurses and patients. It could be a jilted boyfriend of one of the nurses. There's no reason why he shouldn't show up, or, you know, if you're the nurse's therapist, you know . . . we would just take it for granted that her therapist is there to talk to her and so it freed us to make all kinds of fun choices like that and added another layer of richness to it."

Cackowski also compliments his director. "I think [Noah] demands a lot from people and I really like to be challenged and I really like to be pushed to do my best work. I really like to be pushed to play at the top of my intelligence, which is big with him. He emphasizes theme as well, which I think helps elevate long form to art, you know. It was our primary focus of the show of, like, addressing social concerns or, you know, big issues like racism, homophobia, misogyny, what have you, but he would encourage us that if those things came up to not shy away from those and play subtler shadings of things. For example, the version of a racist in a Harold is usually so over the top that it indicates to the audience, 'We know, we definitely don't think this way, this is silly,' you know. It's a Klan-member racist that we can all laugh at, but he encouraged us to find the racist within us, the person who was more believable and more human and therefore scarier and more believable. You know, that they're not cartoonish, so that was kind of a cool thing as well."

The form in *Close Quarters* was a big hit but such a challenge to improvisational ensemble that no record of another ensemble attempting it in Chicago exists. However, Kevin Mullaney in New York has attempted to direct some shows utilizing the idea of compressed time at the UCB Theater.

## The Movie

The long-form improvisation known as the Movie was popularized by IO house teams the Family and the Tribe at ImprovOlympic in the early '90s. It differed from other long forms taught at the theatre because, rather than being patterned after the Harold with consistent themes and patterns, the Movie was a literal improvised interpretation of the form of a movie.

The players on stage ask for a genre and title from the audience and then improvise the form of a movie as accurately as possible. The Movie follows more of a short-form aesthetic than most long forms, since many of the laughs generated come from predeter-mined gags, and the pace is lightning fast. A recurring bit, for exam-ple, in performances, is that often a player would come from off stage, freeze the scene and lift a player so he or she is horizontal to the stage, proclaiming that the audience is seeing a camera shot from up above.

The long-form exclamation "cut to," which is often used in other forms, originated in the Movie. When two players are doing a scene speaking of a particular moment, a player comes on stage and announces "Cut to: that moment" and we see the moment.

The form is still taught in New York at the UCB Theater but has been extinguished at ImprovOlympic in Chicago, where once an entire level of the training center was devoted to the teaching and perfection of the Movie. Rarely, if ever, has the form been performed in Chicago for the past five years. Whether someone will revive the form in Chicago is doubtful. It is often referred to in a derogatory fashion by long-form improvisers today, since much of it relies on established gags reminding the audience that they're watching a "movie."

## The Bat

ImprovOlympic house team Georgia Pacific created this form in the late '90s. It is a variation on something generally known as the Blind Harold. The Blind Harold would be used mostly in rehearsals and workshop situations as an exercise in listening.

Listening exercises are primary in the formation of the group mind. One of the more well-known is Twenty, or A to Z, depending on whether you choose to employ numbers or letters in the exer-cise. Simply, the group stands in a circle, holding hands, eyes closed, while they run through the alphabet. Anyone can say the next letter (or number) aloud without any sense of pattern. Rather, there is a sense of unity in the group so that each person can sense when someone will (or won't) speak.

Of course, if there's a conflict and two people say a letter (or number) at the same time, the group needs to start over. It can be a difficult, frustrating, but ultimately rewarding exercise. And if the group cheats by finding a pattern that predetermines who's next in line to say a letter, that's one of the Primary Improv Crimes.

Then, the exercise known as the Blind Harold goes one step further. In rehearsals with my old ImprovOlympic team, we would sit in a circle, close our eyes, and simply perform a Harold without seeing anything. Georgia Pacific adapted this into a performance-worthy improvised show in the Del Close Theater, maximizing the dramatics of the form by simply turning all the lights off for the show.

Chris Day, who was a member of Georgia Pacific for over four years, recalls, "[Our coach] Joe Bill had brought it up as a rehearsal piece, to work on listening and stuff. For some reason it really clicked with us. I don't know if we're just a verbal group to begin with and it was a way to play upon our strengths, but it struck a chord in us."

In attempting to bring the Blind Harold into a performance, Georgia Pacific tried to do a forty-minute form on stage, half of which would consist of the Blind element. However, the combination of the blind and the seeing was awkward and Georgia Pacific decided to attempt doing an entire show without any lights at all. The Bat was born.

Day remembers, "At the time we were rehearsing at the Annoyance a lot and they had a room in the basement while they were turning it into a production space. It had nothing in it and it was a small enclosed room with no lights." The form was specifically geared for a Kansas City improv festival, where it was an enormous success. Eventually, Georgia Pacific performed the Bat in complete darkness for a run at the Del Close Theater.

## The Silent Movie

In the year 2000, Chicago Improv Festival producer Jonathan Pitts created what would prove to be a companion form to the Bat. He created a totally improvised Silent Movie. Ensembles had tried in the past to perform silent Harolds and often did them in rehearsals as an exercise in environment and object work, but this would be a more literal stage visualization of what silent movies were in the early twentieth century.

Pitts threw out the idea to people. "If they loved the idea, they were in it," Pitts proclaimed, and the project was prepared for his Around the Coyote Festival. The Silent Movie consisted of two short "films," one a traditional slapstick silent comedy and the other a melodrama, the intention of which was "not a parody," according to Pitts, but rather a re-creation.

The short "films" were improvised sans dialogue in a round white spotlight shone on them by an actual projector that ran without actual film. A flashlight was used to represent close-ups and the iris that was so common in the early days of film. Also, typical plot elements of early popular films were integrated into the meat of the form.

For example, in silent melodramas, babies seemed to die all the time. In the early twentieth century, infant mortality was far, far higher than it is now and one of the more tragic elements of the melodramas of the day. This element was not worked into all the shows, but the cast was still made aware of this and other conventions of the form. And there was, of course, piano accompaniment.

The cast also wore black-and-white and gray costumes and wore black-and-white makeup, giving this form much more of a theatrical nature than the vast majority of improv done in the city, whose props and costumes usually consist of two chairs.

The suggestion consists of a title, specifically for a melodrama and a comedy, and then the audience is entertained for a couple of minutes by a wacky Vaudeville sort (again mirroring exactly what audiences of silent movies got: a combination of live performance and film) while the cast hammers out a couple of beats in the back. Finding the beats briefly may be a betrayal of what some purists would believe is "true" improvisation, but it's necessary in this silent form.

## Montage

A Montage is the most generic of all forms. Its definition is best explained as "a series of scenes following a suggestion." There is little or no regard to themes and patterns. The scenes could be related to each other. They might not be related to each other. Some Montages posing as Harolds are simply Montages with openings, some would say.

Plenty of improvisers will tell you that a Montage is a long form, simply by virtue of the fact that it can go as long as you want without an audience suggestion, and that patterns inevitably emerge even when you're not trying to do so. Patterns pop up subconsciously in the minds of both the performers and the audience, a natural phenomenon, given so many performers in Chicago have studied the Harold at one time or another.

Also, according to some that studied the Harold with Del Close in workshops at the Second City before he joined Charna Halpern, what we call the Montage now used to be what Close called the Harold, before the IO structure took hold.

## Sybil

Andy Eninger recalls, "For me, I've never had the official long-form training. I've never gone to IO. I've learned it from people who have, so I've never had any preconceived rules, so I have a naïve take on long form, so I think it's anything goes. Long form is this whole language, which is continually reinventing itself.

"If the English language was infinite, it's as if every conversation invented another word. You can represent anything in a theatrical way. Can you hit it expressionistically, Brechtian by addressing an audience? In any moment, you can go anywhere."

Eninger's contribution to the long-form fabric of Chicago is something he calls Sybil, a variation (although accidental) of Del Close's Solo Harold. After *Night of the Mutant Harolds,* the Solo Harold was not performed at all and Eninger's form became the dominant one-person long-form improvisation employed in Chicago in the late 1990s.

The origins of Sybil were accidental. A member of Chicago Comedy Company, Eninger and fellow CCC member Kathy Bianchi found themselves alone for a show at the Playground in late 1997. They decided, rather than employing the tried-and-true Chicago tradition of beckoning other improvisers in the house to join them, to go ahead and do the show themselves. Up until that point, "tiny ensemble" improv was very rare. The show was quite accidentally a big hit with the audience, and Eninger and Bianchi decided to work on this long form of introducing many multiple characters between the two of them in a La Ronde–type form. They called it Sybil and had a number of performances under this moniker.

However, Bianchi soon left for Europe and then Eninger took a self-improvement course, where, Eninger recalls, "the class asked that you make goals and challenges for yourself and I chose to do a fully improvised multicharacter one-person show."

He asked his fellow Chicago Comedy Company player Tim Schuenemann to direct him through rehearsals. He resurrected the Sybil name and rehearsed with Schuenemann for one and a half to two months. "It's a whole new language of improv," Eninger says.

Eninger explains some of the steps he ran through in the rehearsal process: "I had to get back to the basics of give-and-take and all that. I had to have very physical characters so that it's easy for the audience to differentiate the body language of different people within the same one person. I had to create a vivid environment to play with, giving yourself a real playground.

"It's the perfect improv training in terms of giving gifts because the only person I would screw was myself. You're trying to be in the moment and plot at the same time."

Performing it gives you "the strange ability to be on stage alone and know that everything is going to be fine."

In performing Sybil, Eninger literally takes the physical place on stage of each character he is playing in the course of normal everyday improv scenes like you see in a long-form show anywhere in Chicago. If he plays a mother and son having a conversation in the kitchen, the player will take the physical place of the mother in the scene, either during her dialogue or sometimes when she is just making a silent reaction to the son. When the focus of the scene turns to the son, whether he is speaking or not, the player jumps to the position of the son, takes on the characteristics of the son immediately, and takes the focus.

"It's completely exhausting," says Eninger. "But there's a point where you get past it. It becomes not really masturbatory. You think you don't have enough for twenty minutes but then you realize how much you hold back."

Once he had a few performances under his belt, Eninger believed "the next level was teaching it, the place where I knew it would push me further. In looking for a place to workshop Sybil as a form for other people to perform, the Playground was very receptive to the idea. Megan Pedersen from the Playground Theater worked with me to set up a format of workshops and shows called

Sybilization." As part of that theatre's Director's Series, which had showcased improvisational works directed by Jason Chin and Rob Mello among others, the theatre presented several "Sybils" performed by Eninger and others who had taken workshops with them.

For Sybil, you get a suggestion from the audience, and then use that word to open the show. Much like Harold, some wordplay, somewhat poetic, lets the performer riff off various ideas. Then a monologue from the point of view of the first character occurs. Then, the structure moves about in a La Ronde–like fashion, the first character interacting with a second character, then the second character interacting with a third, and so on.

Eninger relates, "There's a kinetic energy of bouncing back and forth between characters. Much more I perform the Sybil as a series of monologues with two- to five-person scenes interspersed. It's so funny to see people so strict to the form after I teach it."

In establishing ownership of a form, improvisers will continue to attempt to expand the ideas of what people can accomplish in improvisation. Others have gone even further, using other theatrical methods and more outlandish attempts to do something new and following are some examples of some of the more unique long-form improvisational methods that have come about in the last five years.

# 6 Meisner and Improv

One of the criticisms directed at long-form improvisation in the
'90s was that despite all the talk about truth in comedy, there
was still a multitude of ensembles in Chicago that did the same
exact kind of quick, admittedly funny bits that you would see at a
short-form franchise like ComedySportz. Much of this is the para-
dox of having to perform in a cabaret or bar environment where
the patrons are often loud and obnoxious and the performers
sometimes have to match their level of hysteria in order to even be
heard.

Two improvisers who directly reacted to this criticism were
Kevin Mullaney and Rob Mello. In 1996 in Chicago, Mullaney pro-
duced and Mello directed a long-form show called *Naked,* starring
Stephnie Weir (now seen on *Mad TV*) and Jim Carrane.

Rob Mello is a former dancer whose body "gave out" at the age
of twenty-seven, at which point he began to dabble in improvisational theatre by studying at ImprovOlympic. After studying and
performing there for about five years, Mello says, he "got sort of
dissatisfied with improv and that's when I got back into acting."
Feeling that improvisers were recycling their old bits over and over

again, Mello wanted to delve into something deeper. From that he found the works of Sanford Meisner.

In acting classes back in college, Mello had studied a little of the methods of Sanford Meisner. Meisner was one of the most famous acting teachers of the twentieth century, someone, according to Mello, who had become disenchanted with the Method, popularized by Lee Strasberg, with whom Meisner worked. The Method concentrated on the actor looking inward for inspiration, drawing on her own past experiences to find the emotion required in scenework. For example, one of the popular ways for an actor to find the emotion in a scene of someone close to him dying on stage is to remember what he was thinking and how he felt when someone close to him died in real life. Meisner wrote, "Actors are not guinea pigs to be manipulated, dissected, let alone in a purely negative way. Our approach was not organic, that is to say *healthy*" (*www.sanfordmeisner.com*).

Strasberg and Meisner were founders of the Group Theatre, a theatre ensemble co-op that became one of the most influential cultural centers of theatre in the 1930s, a group at least as fervent in their political and social beliefs as the Compass players would be twenty years later. At that time, Meisner performed in many notable productions like *The House of Connelly, Men in White, Awake and Sing,* and *Paradise Lost.* While still acting with the Group Theatre, he became the head of the acting department of New York's Neighborhood Playhouse School of Theater.

In 1941, the Group Theatre folded and Meisner devoted himself primarily to teaching at the Neighborhood Playhouse, only acting sparingly over the remaining years of his life on film and Broadway. Meisner stayed with the Neighborhood Playhouse for forty-eight years.

Growing out of the days with the Group Theatre and the theories of Constantin Stanislavsky, Meisner created a series of exercises for actors.

He believed acting was about reproducing honest emotional human reactions. What transpired for the actor, according to Meisner, was an "experiment" on stage and the actor's job was to prepare for that experiment. According to Meisner, his approach was designed "to eliminate all intellectuality from the

actor's instrument and to make him a spontaneous responder to
where he is, what is happening to him, what is being done to him"
(*www.sanfordmeisner.com*).

To Meisner, all acting was spontaneous regardless of whether
there was a physical script on hand and the words were placed in
the actors' mouths.

According to the Sanford Meisner Center website, "the primary
tool Meisner employed in preparing his students was spontaneous
repetition. Among his many exercises was one in which two actors
looked directly at each other and one would described a feature of
the other. After this, the two actors would simply say the phrase
back and forth. Because the phrases (such as, 'You have soft eyes')
came from a physical reality apparent to the actors, the statement
retained meaning no matter how often they were repeated. Another
example of Meisner's method has two actors enter a room playing
specific roles without specific lines. They begin to speak and the
plot is formed out of nothing but the surroundings. The actor's con-
cern is to remain in character. Techniques such as these allow actors
to move beyond the printed script and address the underlying emotional or philosophical themes of a play."

Gregory Peck said of Meisner, "What he wanted from you was
truthful acting . . . He was able to communicate, and the proof of
that is the number of people that have come out of [the Neighborhood Playhouse] over a forty-year period who've gone on to become people who set standards of acting" (*www.sanfordmeisner.com*).

With this philosophy of truthful reaction, an application
of Meisner's techniques to Chicago-style improvisational theatre
seemed a natural fit.

Rob Mello comments, "Meisner is also an incredible reality-
based technique. He says something about 'Don't look out the
window when you're on a set and imagine you see a forest and trees
because what you're really going to see is the stage manager.'"
Studying the Meisner technique at Center Theater in Chicago,
Mello was immediately drawn to the naked truth being shown on
stage. Both he and Kevin Mullaney took Meisner technique classes
at the Center Theater, where they were particularly intrigued by the
repetition exercise and how they could use that and other techniques in an improvisational setting.

"It's all based on the simple principle that you are the best thing you can bring to the stage and to be honest up there and that in order to be honest you have to be willing to own all the emotions in front of other people," says Mello.

What he calls "Chicago-style Meisner" fits the city's theatrical reputation as swaggering, intensely emotional, reactionary. And Mello saw Meisner as a good fit for long-form improvisation, a movement that Mello saw as reaching a stage of stagnation.

"I thought improv was not meeting its potential as an art form," Mello explains. "I had grown past the stage when I wanted to get laid and get laughs and I found that there was all this yappity yap about 'truth in comedy.' There was a lot of lip service paid to this truth stuff—you gotta be honest, you gotta be real—and they would pay this lip service to this in class but when you got on stage it would get thrown out the window and it would become jokey.

"[I think] really what they're saying is rather than being dishonest and doing a scene about a gigantic snail with human hands, be honest and just do a scene about another person. I think that's the concept of truth in comedy. Or be truthful and do a scene about a marriage that's falling apart. That's honest or for me, I was like, the situation is honest but it's not *all* necessarily honest."

When Mello was first studying at ImprovOlympic, he says, "I remember being really turned on by the Family and when they were doing the Harold. There were connections and their patterns and their explorations of a theme, more like performance art. It was chaos but it made perfect sense. It had some integrity to it."

Mello continues, "[But] the Movie ruined improv. It gave even more outside things for the improvisers to use and to rely upon to not have to do good scenes because you could get a laugh just by saying 'cut to' and then doing something wacky and then some film technique that the audience is entertained by."

Jim Jarvis, another improv director who studied Meisner-based techniques at Center Theater, says, "People go into improv wanting to be funny. Deep down inside, improv is about being vulnerable and not *having* to be funny. This is what you need to do to be a good actor. You need to be vulnerable on stage."

Rob Mello explains how he and Kevin Mullaney ended up doing the show *Naked*. "How it really started," says Mello, "was that

Jimmy Carrane lived in the neighborhood of the bar I worked at and would come and hang out and get whatever free beverages and food he could get from me, and he would hang out."

Mello remembers, "I think I had the idea of two people doing an hour-long scene. And when I asked Kevin to produce it, I think Kevin said, 'Let's use some of the Meisner,' and I think before then I had already started playing with repetition in rehearsals [with Harold teams at ImprovOlympic]. Kevin also wanted to integrate other aspects of the technique that was being taught at the Center Theater that I wasn't familiar with. I think he brought that aspect of it in."

Mullaney relates, "Repetition at Center Theater was a very raw experience. It was some of the most real stuff I ever did on stage. It really got you to do stuff. Yeah, people were making out in repetition. But you couldn't actually harm anyone. There were certain guidelines but there were very few.

"You couldn't physically harm someone. You could threaten them. You could intimidate them, you could say whatever you wanted, but you couldn't actually harm them and you couldn't have intercourse and you couldn't—I think the third one was you couldn't defecate. There may have been a legitimate reason to pee on stage but there's no legitimate reason to actually defecate on stage."

Repetition, as taught at Center Theater and by Mello, Mullaney, and the new generation of practitioners in improv, is at its purest essence incredibly simple, yet terribly intimidating once you're in the middle of it.

Two people are on stage facing each other. One person begins with a one-word description of how she feels about that other person at that certain moment. For example, you may not normally be sexually attracted to someone in your normal, everyday life, but in repetition you look for that one moment you *are* sexually attracted to that person, or angry or indifferent or smugly looking down upon him.

In a single word, you say what you feel (aroused, irritated, etc.) *or* you project what you sense the other person is feeling. Whether you are speaking of your own feelings or what you believe your partner's feelings are is usually indicated by something as simple as pointing either at yourself or the other person. The same is returned by the other person, and your words may repeat over and over again, or else what you feel may evolve as a reaction to what the other person is saying.

An example:

PERSON A:  Love

PERSON B:  Disgusted

PERSON A:  Love

PERSON B:  Disgusted

PERSON A:  Hurt

PERSON B:  Indifferent

PERSON A:  Hurt

PERSON B:  Indifferent

PERSON A:  Angry

PERSON B:  Indifferent

PERSON A:  Angry!!

PERSON B:  Don't care!!!

PERSON A:  Angry!!!

In an exchange like this, blows can result. Person A might push Person B down on the ground. Off stage, the actor who is portraying Person B is probably not universally disgusted by the love that Person A is feeling, but rather just feeling that emotion in that particular moment.

This is an exchange that can take less than a minute (or whenever the director decides to stop you), but everything that each person is feeling and reacting to depends wholly on the other person. Your partner is the single most important thing on that stage and you need to heighten and add to everything your partner says and does.

Rob Mello explains that "the reason we banter that one word back and forth is to get you out of your head so that you're not trying to think of what to say next.

"It also really helps sharpen your impulses. It is also designed to give you choices. I can be in a scene and be angry at someone and also be sexually attracted to them and then I can choose because no one has *one* pure thing; I can choose which one I'm gonna go with, or am I gonna go with them together? Mr. Meisner's repetition as I understand it was a little bit different from the Chicago style, in that Mr. Meisner's was, you know, 'I'm wearing a brown shirt.' 'You're . . .' And yes it does get more visceral than that but I think the Chicago style really focuses on *attracted, hate, love,* not so much about someone's shoes."

"One of the things," Kevin Mullaney remembers, "that Rob wanted to do with *Naked* that I thought was really overdue was I think most people were looking at improv and trying to find new tricks for improv to do. 'What if we did it and we did it like this and we had this many scenes and we went backward in time and we did *this* and we did *this?*' And Rob really aggressively took a step in the other direction, saying, 'No, let's take all the tricks away and just do scenes. Let's take all the little cut-to's and tagouts and other things that people have figured out over the years, that entertains an audience in a way—makes long-form improv work—take all those things away and just do a scene.'"

Repetition was not the only exercise utilized in the rehearsal process for *Naked*. Mello explains, "We did what were called setups, which is something they do at Center Theater. A setup . . . is used primarily for you to create any character you want to create and you also put yourself in a scenario; so for instance, one of my setups I remember doing was, 'I have incurable brain cancer and I'm going to kill myself.'"

The setup itself utilized a character release, which is simply a monologue by the improviser, often answering questions from the director, all about the character. Her loves, her hates, her history, all the people in her life, the big events of her life, everything that makes up a character. Mello continues, "You always want high stakes. 'I'm killing myself in the next hour and fifteen minutes' so I would sit there and do a release in character, telling my whole story, blah blah blah. The teacher would poke into your preparation, whether they buy that you have cancer, and stuff like that, that you're emotionally *full.* The other people are listening, they hear the story and then they send in the 'neighbor.'"

Mello says, "You usually have someone else involved in it. You'll say, 'My girlfriend is coming over in fifteen minutes. I'm going to kill myself. I'm chopping up arsenic. I'm going to put it in my drink, while my girlfriend is here and without me telling her, I am going to drink this arsenic because I want to die because of my cancer but I don't want to die alone. And I don't want to tell her because I don't want her to stop me.'

"So the reason why a *neighbor* goes in rather than another student playing the girlfriend is that I as an actor might have cast someone in my head as the girlfriend so then I suddenly have to accept that Joe Blow is my girlfriend when I've cast someone in my head. I've done preparation around someone else being my girlfriend. So then they improvise together, I would step out of the room and the neighbor does a little release, why Rob's stupid for wanting to kill himself. I'm coming over to stop him. How am I going to stop him? I'm going to do *X, X,* and *X.*

"And it's used in the Chicago-style technique to engage the imagination, to have you practice on character preparation. It's practice on character preparation because you get to choose the character so you can work very close to home so you can get in the habit of working very close to home so that when you get handed a character from a play you can figure out how to find your way.

"So we did a few setups, with either of them [Carrane and Weir] playing the neighbor and then at a certain point we just started running hour-long scenes. The reason why it's not a one-act play—I didn't want to call it a one-act play because I didn't want it to become about them necessarily finding conflict and resolution. When we were talking about it, it was always use the concept of a foreign film of, like, it's a character study. It's two people sharing an hour together. Something might happen, nothing might happen. So we did setups."

Sometimes Carrane and Weir would simply do character releases on their own without the setups. Jim Jarvis says, "It's sitting down and doing a release. Developing a character. Who broke your heart? What's the most painful experience you ever had?" An improviser would take center stage and simply do a character monologue punctuated by questions from the fellow improvisers sitting in the audience.

"All of a sudden they have to dig deep inside," says Jarvis. "Drop into that character and do character-based monologues. Surface-wise . . . how do you feel?" Releases, while not involving two improvisers on stage, used the improviser's emotions and imagination to fuel a character. This kind of releasing does run counter to Meisner's teachings, but those who direct improv using Meisner's techniques believe these accompany the other exercises well.

In improv classes in Chicago, virtually no attention is paid to the picture of the actor on stage. Rarely, if ever, are improvisers told how to breathe on stage, how to project their voices, stand up straight. So much is concentrated on the rules of improvisation that what's lost are the basic tenants of acting in front of an audience. Of course, one of the dangers of using these methods is that it gets the improvisers in their heads, so directors like Mello and Jarvis will often only use these tools in rehearsals and shows with improvisers who have long been through the improv training centers and have become comfortable enough and instinctive enough in their improv methods that they're able to concentrate further on their theatricality.

All these methods were used in the rehearsal process of *Naked*. However, there were pitfalls in presenting a show that consisted of a single hour-long scene. Even at ImprovOlympic, where the finest improvisers have studied and performed for twenty years, there is still an assumption made by the audience that what they're about to see is supposed to be funny. That is also the assumption made by students and performers.

Despite the danger of audience expectation, according to Mello, one of the greatest challenges of presenting a single hour-long scene with no audience suggestion was "that when you were even remotely sort of jokey, it stood out like a sore thumb."

"So you had to be, like, really careful, so when the overall piece started to resemble a regular improv scene, it would stick out so poorly, because three minutes earlier there was something really touching and beautiful and very honest and simple. Jim Carrane, I remember, introduced something into one of the shows where he was going to be—I don't know—a *nacho cheese salesman* or something, just something stupid, so you don't have any room to make that kind of false choice or something like that, or silly choice. I can't do an hour on nacho cheese chips."

Another challenge "was trying to remind the audience that it was improvised because it's worthless unless you realize it's improvised. Otherwise, you're going like, 'This is sort of a poorly written one-act!'"

Mello recalls, "What I didn't like was, in retrospect—I have so much more knowledge now that I think I could make it work and I think I got frustrated at it—what I didn't like (they did very brave work at the time, don't get me wrong) but there's always where they weren't quite willing to go way over the edge.

"They're way over the edge for normal improv. They're kissing on the mouth. There's the occasional tear, but [they're] not quite feeling confident enough to give some of those really breakthrough breathtaking scenes that you see in plays (I know. It wasn't a play), like someone having a complete meltdown, or becoming really sexual, or becoming . . . those opportunities would present themselves, so I didn't like that I don't think it really met its full potential. And I get frustrated, because if it doesn't meet its full potential then it needs a form, then it needs a plot, I think if it's not really raw it's got to have something to back it up a little bit. That's what I thought was wrong with *Drive,* another one of my famous and formless shows."

*Drive,* produced at the Playground Theater in the fall of 2000 as part of their Director's Series, was Mello's attempt at directing a totally improvised show utilizing the Meisner technique with a large ensemble. "I wanted to work on Meisner in a group setting, sweated over form but went back to repetition. Ninety-five percent of the cast I think got it."

Other missed opportunities presented themselves during the run of the show. Mello recalls, "There's one scene that stands out in my mind, Christine is talking to David, who's under her sink fixing her plumbing and there's sort of a sexual tension between them. I can see that there's every impulse in her body to mount him and she doesn't do it, and to me it was the same thing where they don't quite go far enough to really make it stick."

In attempting to get improvisers to go with their impulses more often, Mello continues to teach Meisner classes, as well as Meisner classes that are directly intended for improvisers. He has also held one-night "open repetition," in which anyone is invited to participate in an evening of repetition exercises. Improvisers who are very experienced with repetition get to do the exercises with improvisers who are new, and it is a good way to introduce yourself to the practice.

Whether or not the uses of Meisner in improv will ever catch on widely in Chicago remains to be seen. The attraction of improvisers to more and more wacky comic antics would dispel any belief that truly emotionally engaging improvisational theatre will prove to be popular. Perhaps, however, shows like *Naked* and *Drive* may end up inspiring a new group of young improvisers to really use their art form to say things that are important to them—just like the Compass players.

# 7　Narrative Long Form

While many Chicago students of improv attempt long form based on the principles of the Harold, others are more ambitious in the context of telling a fully realized improvised story in one or two acts. After the Compass dabbled in scenario plays in the 1950s, integrating improvisation into predetermined stories, the idea of long-form improvisation came about in Chicago in the mid-'80s, when the Harold at ImprovOlympic was first taking off.

While Charna Halpern and Del Close were changing the improv world, other companies were experimenting not with Haroldesque pieces, but work more closely tied to the scenario plays. A company called Instant Theater, which featured Homer Simpson-to-be Dan Castellaneta, did scenarios in Chicago in the mid-'80s. They directly used the scenario play after participating in workshops with David Shepherd in 1982. Said Instant Theater codirector Deb Lacusta, "Of all the improv work we did, the stuff that most intrigued myself and Dan was the scenario work we did with David. A bunch of us who had studied with David all got together. We were tired of doing the sketch stuff, because you can only take it so far."

Second City director and teacher Michael Gellman, who is credited with coining the term *long-form improvisation,* mounted experimental one-act improvisations at CrossCurrents when Improv-Olympic was also performing there. According to a 1986 article in the *Chicago Tribune*—the first time the burgeoning long-form movement got any press—audience members who attended Gellman and company's show gave the actors the where's written down on slips of papers, locations that would elicit emotions of some kind in the actors. From there the actors would improvise for one act.

Plenty of other shows have experimented with one-act improvisation as well, but getting an improvised two-act show up was, in Chicago critic Jack Helbig's words, the "Holy Grail." Two shows—among others—in Chicago in the past five years have attempted to create a two-act improvised experience, one in essence a musical adaptation of the scenario play, the other an attempt to integrate mythic story structure into an improvised two-act show.

## Sheila's Instant Odyssey

The improv group known as Sheila was born at the University of Chicago. Second City cofounder Bernie Sahlins helped start a sketch and revue ensemble consisting of University of Chicago undergraduates called Off Off Campus. Some of those performers, upon graduation, formed the group Sheila, which began a weekly run at Jimmy's Woodlawn Tap in Hyde Park, where many Compass performances occurred in the '50s.

Edmund O'Brien was an alumnus of Off Off Campus who joined Sheila in the fall of 1992. O'Brien remembers, "Jimmy's is a great place because the audience is very diverse. It's part of the University of Chicago crowd, part of the Hyde Park community. A large percentage of the audience comes back every week, [which] really forced us to start to . . . you couldn't rely on getting away with gimmicky schtick because you had the same audience every week." In a similar vein to the days of the Compass players at the University of Chicago in the 1950s, the humor also had to be intelligent. Sheila could not and did not rely on bathroom humor.

For most of the group, their studies with Off Off Campus were their only exposure to improvisation and thus they were

*Figure 7–1: Sheila's Instant Odyssey* Photo by Kenneth Lee

not aware of what was going on in long-form improvisation at ImprovOlympic and other theatres on the North Side of Chicago. Rather, they were taught improvisation as a rehearsal tool for writing revues.

O'Brien says, "We thought Harold was something that was longer than a three-minute scene, and the only long form we knew was, like, a one-act play, so when we decided to do a 'long form' we would do a twenty- or thirty-minute improvised one-act play.

"We saw ourselves as people who brought improv back to Hyde Park. We wanted to deal with it theatrically and weren't worried about laughs in the one-act." For the next two years, through personnel changes that occurred because various members moved to New York or Los Angeles to hit it big, Sheila settled on a five-person ensemble that decided, after two years of performing at Jimmy's, that they would try a closed run of a show on the North Side of Chicago, where most long-form improvisation thrived.

This show was titled *Sheila's Giant Wall of Plot Twists.* Opening in the spring of 1994 in the shadow of Wrigley Field for an eight-week run of late Saturday nights, the show was such a success it ended up running for two years. A variation on Shakespeare's plot twists, the Giant Wall consisted of thirty sheets of paper, numbered one to thirty, each with a different plot twist inside. The improvised act would proceed until a player would yell "Freeze!" and the audience would yell out an appropriate number, each one covering another twist. The plot twists ran the gamut from "an enemy approaches" to "a secret is revealed."

O'Brien believed by having audience suggestions occur throughout the show and keeping the audience more involved in the process of guiding the improvisations, they would enjoy the show that much more.

Following their successful two-year run, during which time they still performed at Jimmy's every week, Sheila became a founding member of the Playground Theater, lending an air of legitimacy to the new improv co-op. Having open runs at the North Side venue as well as Jimmy's was a good way to keep their practices fresh while they schemed for ways to follow up the Giant Wall with another closed-run show on the North Side.

O'Brien asked, "What was the next step? We dabbled with some idea of written stuff but weren't all writers and the best thing they did was improv and then decided to tackle instead the fully improvised two-act play."

New member David Stern was still an undergraduate at the University of Chicago and had been studying mythology quite a bit. He introduced to the group the concept of the twelve-step mythic story structure popularized by author Joseph Campbell. He and the rest of Sheila decided that by integrating that structure into an improvised piece, it was possible to create a fully improvised two-act play.

Although they had settled on the structure, O'Brien said it "was by far the hardest thing any of us had ever done and I've never done anything that hard since. It was very frustrating, because after improvising for seven years, feeling very comfortable on stage, it was like learning improv all over again because we were all in our heads constantly."

In preparing for the conceptual phase of rehearsal, each member of Sheila read a book called *The Writer's Journey* (1998) by Christopher Vogler. The book is intended for screenwriters, to let them in on the twelve-step, three-act story structure of the hero's journey. In adapting the structure for an improvised two-act play, the group was able to use the concepts behind these beats in building an improvised piece. While they would not necessarily follow the mythic steps to the letter, it created a foundation around which they could create the improvised play. The belief is that the mythic story structure is the basis for the majority of stories that have ever been told. The best modern example on film of the mythic story structure is most likely the original *Star Wars*.

Within this structure, Sheila added another parameter in which they needed to play in order to make the play palatable for audiences. O'Brien and company decided that the audience had to like their hero. Says O'Brien, "No one wants to see a miserable bastard for ninety minutes."

Rather than getting multiple suggestions from the audience, Sheila only asked for a common gathering place from the audience. This common gathering place would end up being part of the ordinary world.

The group then followed the twelve steps of the Hero's Journey, always realizing it is there in the two-act play:

### 1. Hero is introduced in the Ordinary World

Using the *Star Wars* example, the ordinary world is that place where the hero sits restless, yearning for adventure. Luke Skywalker sits in the desert, bored stiff on a moisture farm. (One thing to consider in these examples is that the mythic story structure does not necessarily only follow adventure stories where there is a clearly defined hero. Often, that structure can be found in romantic comedies, and just about anything else.)

### 2. Receive the Call to Adventure

As Vogler explains in his book, "The hero is presented with a problem, challenge, or adventure to undertake" (Vogler 1998, 15). It doesn't always have to be something particularly dramatic, like a treasure hunt.

### 3. Refuse the call

Although our hero yearns for adventure, he is still a prisoner of the ordinary world. When called to adventure, Luke Skywalker decided to not follow Obi-Wan Kenobi to rescue the princess.

### 4. Mentor
And it is Kenobi that is the mentor in *Star Wars*. The mentor knows the hero's potential and encourages him or her.

### 5. Cross the first threshold
Now, encouraged by the mentor, the hero embarks on the adventure.

### 6. Tests, allies, and enemies
Once the hero embarks on the adventure the sixth step can take up the majority of the storytelling—the meat of the storytelling. On a literal journey or road trip, these are the various foibles that occur on the way to achieving the quest. In *Star Wars*, it's the various obstacles (like the aliens in the cantina or the Tie Fighters) that pop up in our hero's quest for the princess.

### 7. Approach the inmost cave
Then the "inmost cave" is when the hero first approaches the object of his quest. This is the point in *Star Wars* in which our hero finds out the princess is in the giant Death Star and within reach.

### 8. Supreme ordeal
In a romantic comedy, the supreme ordeal would be when our hero and the object of her affection finally go out on the first date, which is an incredible disaster and it looks like the couple that is meant for each other will never get together. Or in an adventure story, our hero is dropping headfirst down a cliff after being thrown off by the enemy. Luke Skywalker and his friends are on the verge of getting mashed in a trash compacter. It is the cliffhanger.

### 9. Hero takes possession of her reward
After facing certain death, either literally or figuratively, the hero celebrates her victory. This is not the final victory, but it is the key to victory she often achieves. Our hero in *Star Wars* escapes the Death Star with princess in hand.

### 10. The road back
Vogler explains in his book, "The hero's not out of the woods yet. We're crossing in to Act Three now as the hero begins to deal with

the consequences of confronting the dark forces of the Ordeal" (Vogler 1998, 23). This is the point at which Skywalker realizes he has to return to the Death Star and destroy it.

### 11. The third threshold and resurrection

This is the second life-and-death experience for the hero, at which point he may actually appear to have perished in the battle but becomes transformed by the experience. Luke Skywalker destroys the Death Star using the Force rather than the technology at hand that would help him find the tiny target through which his missile must go.

### 12. Return with the elixir

The "Elixir" is the prize or final lesson the hero wins upon her return to the Ordinary World. In the case of the romantic comedy, it's when the two leads have their wedding. In *Star Wars,* the Death Star is destroyed and Luke and his comrades are presented with unsightly necklaces in a big ceremony.

The mythical story structure does not fall that far from scenes and stories that Sheila would have ordinarily told without knowledge of this structure. Much of what defines the mythic story structure is what goes on subconsciously when people tell stories. There is a protagonist, there is a goal, and there are conflicts that come up that threaten the goal. One can say it is as lightly drawn a sketch as the Harold as it is first taught in classes. When one looks at the twelve steps and then looks at various films that either consciously or unconsciously follow the structure, one can realize that there is often some part of this structure in *every* story.

Also, what Sheila had to study in Vogler's book was the idea of the archetype. The hero, the mentor, and other characters in the hero's journey are archetypes, which Vogler describes as "ancient patterns of personality that are the shared heritage of the human race" (Vogler 1998, 29). These ancient patterns exist in each one of us.

The most important consideration of the Hero's Journey, just like many other long forms that have developed over the past twenty years, is that it exists as a framework. Like O'Brien said, the danger of doing a two-act is to get too much in your head. If the scenes do not follow the Hero's Journey specifically, they probably still do subconsciously. Not every story sticks to the model like *Star Wars* does.

The show that sprung from Sheila's experiments with the mythic story structure was *Sheila's Instant Odyssey.* It ran for two separate eight-week runs. Reviews were enthusiastic. The *Chicago Tribune* proclaimed that "the Sheila Theater Group successfully assembles four audience suggestions into an 80 minute hero's journey . . . the deft sextet, apart from consistently witty banter and fertile running jokes, pulled off a rare trick for Chicago improv: They kept the story very real without taking themselves too seriously" (Jones 1997).

After the two runs of *Sheila's Instant Odyssey,* the group still did shows at Jimmy's Woodlawn Tap and the Playground until they had their final shows at both locations in June 2001, calling it a day after nearly a decade, when O'Brien and wife packed it up to move to L.A.

Whether or not Sheila found the Holy Grail of improv when they used the mythic story structure, it was perhaps the most noteworthy attempt to create an improvised two-act play in recent Chicago history.

## Musical Improv

When I was taking classes at ImprovOlympic just a few short months after their Clark Street theatre opened, the Harold shows had a very specific format. The show would consist of two Harold teams, opening with the two teams appearing together on stage in a game called Musical Option. Then the first team would perform their Harold, which usually took anywhere between fifteen and thirty minutes, depending on how well they did and where the light booth person thought the set should end. Then, the two teams would converge again (sometimes, if the first team was too new, only the second team would appear) for a game called the Dream, in which an audience member would be asked to volunteer to come up on stage and replay his or her entire day for the players and audience. The players would then re-create what dreams the audience member may have as a result of his or her experiences of that day. Then the second team would go up, and finally at the end, the two teams would reunite for a round of freeze tag.

Musical Option seemed to me to be the game that terrified the most people in those shows. The game was simple in concept. The host would first introduce the game, explaining that a normal scene would occur and that any audience member is invited to yell "Freeze!" and shout out a musical style. It could be disco, blues, country western, skiffle, reggae, or any other musical style you can think of. Then, at different points during the scene, audience members yell "Freeze!" and then a new musical style.

Given such a gimmicky, audience-friendly, "short-form" style, the performances often suffered mightily and eventually the ImprovOlympic dropped the Musical Option game.

However, music and improvisational theatre would not be separated for long. Rather, the ImprovOlympic resident team Baby Wants Candy and an independent production called *Musical! The Musical* would explore all the opportunities that the musical provided. Both showed how musicals could be created improvisationally, how the emotion of the scene becomes so intense that the player or players have no choice but to sing because they have no other way to express just what they feel.

At IO, Baby Wants Candy performs a forty-minute musical three nights a week, the first team at the theatre ever to have a regular gig at the theatre of more than one show a week. The team was originally created by ImprovOlympic veteran Peter Gwinn in December 1995 as an "experimental team," a team with people he invited especially to perform in the Harold Cabaret, all longtime veterans of long-form improvisation at IO. They experimented with various forms with coaches like Rob Mello and Scott Robinson, and it was under Robinson that the team began performing forty-minute musicals.

As described by Justin Seidner in the University of Chicago *Weekly News,* here's how a typical Baby Wants Candy show might go: "Baby Wants Candy began with a chorus line of zoo employees, each taking a line or two of song to tell us about their trials at the zoo (which we later learned was in San Diego). This jazzy piece grew until each actor had sung a few bars, which transitioned well into their first scene. At this point one could begin to appreciate the talents of their accompanist, who did a virtual survey of musical theatre throughout the show.

"The audience was hooked. As the story progressed we learned that the animals disliked the zoo (big surprise), and sought to return to their homeland in Africa, but not before enjoying the sights of San Diego. There was a wonderful song between two lions about their return to the homeland, backed up by a chorus of hopping gazelles and kangaroos."

Under the leadership of Gwinn and musical director Larrance Fingerhut, a musician and composer with a classical background who ended up falling into improvisational theatre accompaniment, Baby Wants Candy has become the premiere team at IO Chicago, winning raves at the Edinburgh Fringe Festival in Scotland and admirers the world over.

In showing improvisers how to improvise musically, Fingerhut says the most challenging thing to teach is that in order to sing a song, a great deal of emotion must be present and the player must be willing to grab all the focus. The character *has* to sing to express what he or she is feeling. Grabbing focus is a hard thing to do for trained improvisers since they are always taught to *give* focus.

Another show, *Musical! The Musical,* attempted to create a *two-act* improvised musical. Not affiliated with any of the long-form improv theatres in Chicago, the show was the creation of Nancy Howland Walker. Walker hails from Boston, where there is not a large long-form improvisational movement. She was with an improv group called Improv Boston.

Says Walker, "In Improv Boston, we did, like, a thirty-minute, forty-five-minute musical as part of our show and we just made it up. We hadn't heard of anyone else doing it, and it was so much fun, it was the part of the show we enjoyed the most and the audience seemed to enjoy the most. It was more gimmicky. Maybe [the musical] was from a story or maybe it was just from a menu or a problem in society, or something. We would also get song types and during it, the musical director would freeze us, 'Freeze! The next show will be Kletzmer! The next song will be Tiny Tim.'"

In coming to Chicago and playing with the Free Associates, Walker became familiar with the scenario-based long-form improvisation popularized in their parodies. Then, Walker became interested in putting up a show that would expand on the half-hour musicals her troupe performed in Boston, creating a two-act musical with improv. "It was so wonderful," remembers Walker. "The universe just opens up and you decide to do something and you really want to and it's coming from a good place, and we found a musician right away: Randy Craig, a fabulously talented guy who really

*Figure 7–2: Musical! The Musical* Photo by Nancy Howland Walker

wanted to do it." They booked the Mercury Theater, a new stage on the North Side, for a late-night run.

Walker continues, "There was a brand-new funding for the arts, a company that started called the Beck Institute. Dave Sinker was hired by them. He was going to give out money although it was more of a loan, gave them ten thousand dollars to start to give them really professional posters and actors. They were able to get really professional posters and graphics.

"Mercury Theater fell through and then we got Royal George prime time, so we were able to do a real theatre run, not an improv run. In fact I didn't put 'improv' anywhere in the advertising or any-thing." Walker believed that the term *improv* attached to a show would create a preconceived notion, especially among critics, for whom *improv* sometimes is just another word for *bad.*

When *Musical! The Musical* ran, the critics unanimously praised the show. Walker says, "It's so exciting. Everyone that's ever been in-volved in it says it's the most challenging, hardest improv they've ever done, but they love it, they just love it."

In rehearsing for the show, Walker and her cast had much to cover in integrating music and improvisation. Walker says, "There's so much, it would be hard to write down! The secret I think is to set up the rhyme so you always think of the last word first. And of course we do exercises to help people do that, but a lot of improvis-ers, they have a hard time with that because they've always been told that you can't think on stage, which is totally not right. . . . You just have to stay out of your head, but you have to think. Some im-provisers really hesitate when it comes to that. So setting up the rhymes, getting over that block first. Besides, improvisers who do blues games or, you know, in the short form, and do musical stuff in that, it's important in that, it's important in all musical improv.

"I teach melody. Because a major thing that a lot of improvisers do, they're thinking so hard about the words that it's all just one thing, you think then it better be brilliant because that's all that the audience will be listening to. Whereas if you calm down a little and put a melody line in there, there's something else to listen to. . . . That's what makes it seem like a real song. It's a little harder these days with popular music, which doesn't really have any melody un-fortunately . . . so the younger people in class have a harder time with that. On the other hand, it's easier to teach, because we are so sophisticated. Our culture listens to music all the time, it's always in the background, we just grow up with it all around, so even people who think, 'Oh, I don't know anything about music. I'll be awful,'—they *do* know. They can hear when the music ends. They're sophis-ticated."

The show itself opens with the players letting the audience know that they are the backers of a new Broadway musical and can shout out the choice of any existing story that they would like to see made into a musical. Oftentimes, it is the biography of a famous person, or an existing play or book or movie. Walker says some of the musicals they've had to do include the life stories of Gandhi, Madonna, Jerry Springer, Jenny Jones, and other challenging fare like musical versions of *Angela's Ashes* and *Death of a Salesman*.

The style that the cast shoots for, Walker says, is modern Broadway, rather than the classic Broadway one sees in shows like *Guys and Dolls* and *Annie Get Your Gun*. "Modern Broadway is just screwy," she explains. "You know, like Sondheim stuff; you can get away with a lot more. Sometimes we'll go into the older-time musicals. It's just that modern Broadway is just darker for the most part. It's much more about the dark mindset of the characters rather than just this funny situation. All the main characters are struggling with something. There's much more angst in the modern musical, which makes it great fun to improvise!"

Walker explains, "After we pull the story, we say, 'This is Broadway, so we may change a little bit of this because they do that on Broadway . . . so sit back and relax, here's the overture.' So as the overture goes on, we have maybe two minutes to decide who starts the opening number. Who plays and what is the main character? We don't always go for the obvious main character."

Sometimes if the audience shouts the name of a show, the performers will choose to focus on a character who was not the focus of the original story. Thus, although *Musical! The Musical* musicalizes many stories that already exist, the players attempt through improvisation to add a twist here and there, not relying entirely on the point of view already established in the original story. Also, not every performer will know the content of the story. Walker points to *Angela's Ashes* as an example of a book that only two performers had read when the audience chose that story to musicalize. In that case, the improvisers are left completely to their own devices.

Through the melding of music and improvisational theatre, both *Musical! The Musical* and Baby Wants Candy explored new territory not seen before in Chicago improv. With the *Instant Odyssey*, Sheila showed the improvised two-act play was possible.

Chicago does not feature a great many improvised shows that attempt to create the one-act or two-act improvised play, but with such a wide variety of talents in Chicago, no doubt more groups will find it necessary to explore improv in a narrative fashion.

# 8     Long-Form POVs

Since the Compass players introduced improvisational theatre to the masses in the 1950s, there have been numerous interpretations on how to present that work to the entertainment-hungry public. For several of the decades that followed the demise of the Compass, it was generally the accepted belief that improvisation was only a rehearsal tool, a process to develop written material.

To improvise . . .
  1. To invent, compose, or perform with little or no preparation.
  2. To play or sing (music) extemporaneously, especially by inventing variations on a melody or creating new melodies in accordance with a set progression of chords.
  3. To make or provide from available materials.

*v. intr.*
  1. To invent, compose, or perform something extemporaneously.
  2. To improvise music.
  3. To make do with whatever materials are at hand.

Specifically, Second City's development of the sketch comedy revue was accepted as the "way to do it" in Chicago. Even as this was the view of the function of improvisation, audiences at Second City were able to experience the immediacy of improv performance in the hour-long set following the written revue every night. Those who did not want to shell out the money for a revue could see the improvised set by itself for free, since Bernie Sahlins, then-owner of the theatre, did not believe in charging patrons for fully improvised sets of material.

This led to the long disagreement between Sahlins and Del Close. The improvised sets would provide a certain modicum of entertainment, but Sahlins believed the unknowns of improvisation were too great to risk charging people for an evening of improvised material. Close, who had created Harold while he directed at the Committee, knew that there was a way to present an evening's improvised entertainment that would be worth the price of admission. Improv *could* be an art form.

If people are to accept that, and the experiences of the last twenty years have shown it is indeed an art form, how do we draw the lines of demarcation between styles and does it even matter? Popular interpretation is that there are two "kinds" of improv: short form and long form. Then, within those two kinds of improv, there are further definitions of short form and long form.

The dissection of improvisation into two camps, short form and long form, is mainly based on the differences in approach between a theatre like ImprovOlympic and a theatre like ComedySportz. The origins of both are based on competitions between teams, but while ImprovOlympic moved on from short-form improv under David Shepherd to long-form improv under Del Close, ComedySportz has pretty much stayed under the umbrella of what is generally accepted as short-form improvisation. Thus, perhaps the best way to define long-form improvisation is to first point out what it is *not*.

ComedySportz is a franchise of improv clubs begun in 1984 by Dick Chudnow in Milwaukee, Wisconsin. He based the concept on Keith Johnstone's Theater Sports franchise, interpreting Johnstone's ideas and changing the name a bit, first to TheatreSportz, which, for obvious reasons, had to be changed again to ComedySportz. Chudnow had previously been a member of Kentucky Fried Theater, best known as the birthplace of Zucker-Abraham-Zucker, the creators of *Airplane* and *The Naked Gun*. The ComedySportz philosophy is quick, funny comedy that's easy to digest.

The format of their shows is simple enough. Two teams of what they call "comedy athletes" play between seven and twelve improv games each. A referee is the moderator, keeping the game going and calling "fouls." One example of the games played in ComedySportz shows, as listed on the ComedySportz website, is Shakespeare, in which a team will improvise a scene in Shakespearian prose, based on an audience suggestion. In Elimination Rap, players create a rap on the spot, trading off each other's phrases, getting thrown out if they fall off the meter or fail to rhyme, etc. In Forward/Reverse the referee sends the scene back and forth at will, as though scanning a scene with a VCR, sending the athletes into a frenzy. There are other traditional improv games like Party Quirks, in which a player is chosen as host of a party, leaves the room, and then the audience gives each guest a wacky attribute like "lungs are made of wood" or "thinks he's Ernest Hemingway." The host then has to come back to the party and guess what wacky attribute each guest possesses.

Each franchise theatre tries to vary the games from show to show to keep things at least interesting for the players, as well as provide audiences a reason to make return visits, since there is not an absolutely rigid set of games in place. At the end of the performance, there's a winning team and a losing team. The most important distinction of short form is that none of the improv games connect in any way whatsoever to any other games. ComedySportz, at last count, has clubs in twenty-six cities across North America. Quite literally, the approach of a place like ComedySportz is to approach improv as more sport than art. Indeed, many of the skills learned by improvisers are honed to such a point that the competitive aspect of improv shows has proven very popular. Short-form shows require just as much skill and heightened awareness as long-form shows, but it is the case in Chicago that people involved in long-form shows look down their noses at short form.

Annoyance Theater founder Mick Napier mocks the whole idea of the split between long and short, saying, "I'm a little more cynical about improv's 'art-form-ness.' I guess that kind of ties in with [the idea of] form. It's embarrassing that this is an art form that is designated by its length. It's either short . . . or long. It's an embarrassing concept to me. 'Short book, long book.' 'Small art, big art.' And then, many of the forms of improvisation are derivative of other mediums." The Movie is specifically a form that directly references, of course, movies. Musical improv is often merely an improvised adaptation of basic musical theatre. It's not to take anything away from the artistic viability of the improvisers and their work, however; just that we are seeing something familiar presented in a different venue.

"I was so happy in college when I didn't know anything and we learned together," says Napier. "It was very valuable. It took a lot of power coming to Chicago because then when I learned the rules I found myself confined. It took a long time to get back to that which did not confine me and when I got back to that, I learned that it had nothing to do with the rules that I learned at all."

ImprovOlympic veteran Noah Gregoropoulos says, "I don't buy into the various debates about improvisation. I think they're silly. Long form, short form, story, not story. It's like if you're making whatever you're doing more than what you set out to do, then you're doing it right.

"I've been in great short-form shows and I've watched and been in shitty long-form shows and short-form shows," he continues. "I think if you go out to do short forms to satisfy the forms and to impress the audience with the fact that you're improvising and fall back on your series of Mad Libs, you're doing it shitty. But if in the middle of Expert Panel, the characters start interacting in a way that is scenic and has emotional weight, hey, that's kind of cool. Sometimes that happens. It's night to night. You might see that happen at ComedySportz. You might see the opposite."

Still, with the audience making suggestions and no real effort made to create scenic improvisation, ComedySportz definitely falls into a different category than ImprovOlympic. While games are the thing at ComedySportz, IO perfected the art of long-form improvisation, something that could best be described very generally as "scenic improvisation," an effort made by the players to create a scene that creates a narrative arc of a beginning, a middle, and an end.

The "training wheels" Harold, which Close and Halpern had students perform at IO, splits these components apart with other scenes and games, to create the pattern that more accomplished

Harold players can create instinctively through the group mind. The beginning of Scene A will unfold, followed by the beginning of Scene B. By the time we return to Scene A and see the middle beat, components of the beginnings of Scene B and Scene C can feel their way into Scene A and vice versa.

In between these scenes are the group games. These games differ from the games one sees at ComedySportz in that the goal in the Harold is to create a kind of game on the spot. When first being trained in the Harold, for example, students have learned a game called Slide Show in which someone initiates a group setting, and he or she is going to show a slide show. Inevitably, various players take position in the middle of the imaginary frame and freeze. The host then has to justify the players in her "photos," saying something like, "This is my Uncle Ned and Aunt Nora in the eye of the hurricane."

The games of Harold, when first learning the form, are as basic as this. But the teachers at ImprovOlympic, as their students become more sophisticated, encourage group games to become far more organic, and not a "set" improv game. So then eventually the form itself becomes so transparent that an audience member isn't able to see the "scenes-game-scenes-game-scenes" structure.

Most other long forms that have been created skip the group games altogether; and others do not split the beginnings, middles, and ends of scenes into their separate beats. (The "begin in the middle" rule still applies here. The first of the three components of the narrative arc can then be thought of as the beginning of the middle, the middle scene as the middle of the middle, and the end scene as the end of the middle. The traditional narrative arc will still be apparent, even if the arc is more thematic.)

These are forms like the Deconstruction and La Ronde and other variations on those that play the scenes as a whole. This does not mean they cannot split individual scenes into three parts like the Harold, but as an accepted norm these long forms follow a more traditional path. Even a simple montage, where patterns are not the goal but the players simply go up on stage and play scenes, can still be considered a long-form improvisation because audience participation exists only at the beginning and the players are playing scenes. Even with these montages, patterns often develop subconsciously. Since the vast majority of long-form improvisers in Chicago have learned the Harold at one time or another, the patterns develop often without the players intending it, which, many would argue, is a true "Committee" Harold anyway.

The rules developed by Del Close, Elaine May, and Theodore J. Flicker have been reinterpreted countless times. Teachers have traditionally introduced those basic rules in introductory classes and added others to create a very simple philosophy that can be taught quickly but needs to be perfected over the course of years: Don't ask questions. Don't deny your partner's reality. Accept and build on what your partner initiates. Don't become mired in storytelling. Play at the top of your intelligence.

How have various theatre companies used their background in improvisation to put up a stage performance? As you read earlier, the Compass Players in the 1950s were attempting to put up theatre in a cabaret environment. Unable to find existing plays that would fit such a relatively rowdy environment, one of the members, Roger Bowens, developed the scenario play.

The scenario play contained scene-by-scene synopses for the actors to follow, what long-form improvisers call beats today. The synopses didn't put too much detail into the actions and allowed the majority of the play to be improvised.

Here's an example of an opening scene in a scenario play written by Elaine May for production at the Compass in the winter of 1955/56:

Scene 1: Home of Ehrlicher Flick somewhere on Kedzie. Mr. Flick sits by the window, shouting and arguing with Mrs. Pualto—a daily argument about the garbage, which both enjoy. Various street sounds, peddlers, mothers calling to children, etc. Wilhemina Flick enters carrying packages, very excited. She has a date that evening with Edward Kite, who teaches in the same school she does. She thinks it may mean a proposal. She begs her father to be presentable and not ruin things for her. If Edward insists on meeting him, to please say "hello" and nothing more. Flick protests that he's a foreman, he knows how to talk to people and Wilhemina leaves the room, exasperated. Voice comes over radio announcing "Success Course": it describes his very problem. He answers voice excitedly as though it were present. Voice gives name and address of school, urges him to "Come today!" and saying "I will" Flick goes to get hat.

This scene is fairly well plotted out, but it was up to the actors to put in their own dialogue improvisationally.

Thus, the scenario play is what some say was the first manifestation of what we call long-form improvisation today. This is the attempt by an ensemble to create a fully improvised experience in front of a paying audience, an audience that goes away from what they see fully satisfied. Of course, as with any art form, there are the inevitable arguments of just how much improvisation in a performed piece constitutes improvisation.

There are a few different schools of thought on this.

For example, Jonathan Pitts, coproducer of the Chicago Improv Festival and a player in the first ImprovOlympic shows, says, "I agree with the first work of what is called 'long form' first began with the Compass Players. The Harold began with Del in San Francisco. The term *long form* was first developed by Michael Gellman and his company TheatreWorks. The first media usage of *long form* was by Jack Helbig.

"Is it improv when you know your beats?" asks Pitts. "Yes, as much as it is improv when you know the pursuit and rules of the game you are playing. As much as it is improv when you know the architecture and structure of the long form you are doing. In jazz, there are two kinds of improv. That which works in and around a basic melody, which the musicians leave the structure of the song to explore the themes of the harmony. The other is what is called freeform jazz. Here, there is no given, set melody/harmony/rhythm, everybody just plays their instrument and out of the chaos, patterns appear.

"Even Lenny Bruce, the great jazz/improv comic, would only improvise five minutes or so of each set. Often, he would start riffing on a comedic routine, go somewhere with it for a while and then return to his written/rehearsed monologue. In summation, 'What is long form?' To alter the old cliché about art: I don't always know what it is, but I know it when I see it."

Nancy Howland Walker conjectures, "With a structured Harold, you know the beats; you know what scene you're coming back to, and when. Is that not improv? I just saw a two-man improv show. The structure was movement opening, monologue, scene based on that monologue, monologue, scene, monologue, scene, etc., etc. . . . They were free within the beats to improvise, but they still knew the exact beats of the show."

Jim Jarvis, an improviser and director who got his start at ImprovOlympic and now perpetuates the teachings of Chicago-style Meisner in Chicago says, "I have always felt that the original long form began with the Compass ensemble. After listening to Del in the old days talk about what they did, I always imagined it as really an unscripted and condensed play."

He continues, "Think about it in terms of a short play. I believe that long form tells the story of various lives. The scenes are snippets of the people in the improvised play. You have main characters and supporting characters. Usually we see them in a couple different settings (like you would a play) and somewhere in there, we get closure and a conclusion to the play. Yes, it is oftentimes funny (like a comedic play), but the really seasoned and confident improvisers realize it does not need to always be funny: the Family, Blue Velveeta, Jazz Freddy, etc."

Jarvis continues, "I do think that if you outline beats and then improvise your way to each beat, it is still improvisation. You're exploring the characters and the play from point A to B, B to C, etc. You have a framework to utilize, but then you use your skills as an improviser to get to those points and make it rich tableau filled with social implications—hopefully. Or at least one.

"I think that's why beginning improvisers struggle with long form. They don't get it," continues Jarvis. "They don't get the purpose and don't really understand what long form is. They're just out there scrambling to fill in the blanks and the thirty minutes. *Naked* is a great example of two phenomenal improvisers who understand long form and realize they are in the midst of a sixty-minute scene. Same thing with *Close Quarters, Trio,* etc. And that's why every improviser should learn how to act and every actor show learn how to improvise. They are totally intertwined. And having the command of both makes you a much better artist."

Some long-form improvisation attempts to create an evening's worth of comedy using one arc. The arc may be thematic or narrative. And here's where we see how the two parallel movements of long form exist in improv across North America.

1. Theme—Since the late 1960s, Del Close's Harold has attempted to create themes and patterns to create one whole piece. The thematic throughline is often created by the audience through its suggestion. When begun at the Committee,

according to Jonathan Pitts, a philosophically based question posed by an audience member would act as the suggestion. The theme and pattern would act as the answer to the question.

When Harold was adapted by Close and Charna Halpern at ImprovOlympic in the early '80s, the suggestion became more fluid and the theme grew from the set pattern. Then, ImprovOlympic started teaching other forms: the Deconstruction, for one, and the Movie, popularized by the legendary team the Family.

> 2. Narrative—This is an attempt to create a fully improvised play. This could be in the form of a one-act or two-act play, with beats written out like the scenario play, or like *Sheila's Instant Odyssey*. Other attempts have been made to create fully improvised plays without any hint of a structure of beats whatsoever.

The argument on both the thematic and narrative sides is that one—and not the other—is long-form improvisation. The argument can be made, for example, that the Harold *is* long-form improvisation and vice versa.

One can interpret from the final definition that "materials" may simply be the bodies and instincts of the performers. Materials can also consist of the audience suggestion, perhaps a predetermined style, like in Musical Options, or various suggestions given by an audience.

Brian Stack conjectures, "I associate long form with scenework as opposed to fast-paced games that involve lots of audience suggestions.

"Long-form shows, in my experience, usually incorporate some audience suggestions but not the kind of rapid-fire suggestions that one might see at a short-form show like ComedySportz. It seems like the ideal long-form shows tend to emphasize patient scenes, group mind, careful listening, and characterization. While short-form shows can, of course, have similar goals, I've found that the pace is invariably faster in short form and there's more pressure to go for the laughs. That's not a criticism, just an observation."

Like many improvisers throughout the country, Stack remembers, "The first improv I saw and the first improv I performed was short form and game oriented. I lost interest in it over the years but had a great time doing and watching it—experiences I wouldn't trade for anything. I've found long form more rewarding but it bothers me when people write short form off as worthless or artistically bankrupt by definition. It's simply what the people performing it make it. If they treat the audience with respect and play at the top of their intelligence, there's no reason, in my opinion, that short form can't be an art form, too."

Kevin Mullaney, a teacher at the Upright Citizens Brigade Theater in New York, posits, "At some point you are just splitting hairs. I mean we [Frank Booth at ImprovOlympic in Chicago] did a long-form musical in the early '90s where we had some minor things set like the protagonist of the piece should emerge out of the first scene and the antagonist emerges in the second, and we tried to end with a big number where the conflict was resolved.

"I still considered it long form. At what point would it have become short form? I'm not sure. I think long form has likely become riskier as the years have gone on, with people trying forms with less and less set.

"What I've always felt about form is you change the box that you put the scenes into. You put input in and get different output out depending on what's in the box. Well, forms are different boxes. If you do a traditional-format Harold, more like you get certain kinds of scenework. For instance, in group scenes, you get more 'game stuff,' which usually doesn't happen too much in non-Harold forms. I thought that was one of the things that sets apart the Harold, makes it really good, this emphasis on the group game. All kinds of cool things happen in Harold because of that, that don't happen in Deconstructions, that didn't happen in *Naked* and other things. So I've always been interested in form and if you put certain restrictions or certain techniques into someone's head, into a group's head, how is that going to affect the scenework? And I very much like when you take most of the tricks away, what kind of scenework comes out and so on, *but* that's not the whole thing."

Mick Napier says, "When I got to Chicago, I learned about scenic improvisation. That was exciting because I didn't have to improvise under any construct at all, i.e., the construct of a *game* at all. Literally, just hop on stage, get a suggestion, and start talking . . . and that was even more economical for me. So I became a scenic-improvisation kinda guy, never really went back; that's pretty much all I teach now, is scenic improvisation.

"What I say first is 'Fuck it. Do something right away.' Do something. I teach that the best way to start a scene is to attack and take care of yourself.

"[Form is] so derivative to me. Improvisation is human beings standing on stage having no previous information about what they were going to say and making it up," says Napier. "Right now. Everything else under that is derivative to me, and I don't really see the nobility in creating a new improv form. The Chicago Improv Festival just happened, and the Annoyance did a form. We did a big choreographed long form, got one suggestion and it was very choreographed in that transitions were dictated by different moves that people made. I divided it into three different parts, we had a set opening, very choreographed, very, like, 'gay-stylistic.' People moving the same way entering scenes, people transitioning, given different key things that happened in the improv itself, everything triggered by other events, etc., etc., etc.

"All of a sudden, two people would start talking together, or there'd be two two-person scenes going on, two short scenes. Then for no reason, two people would switch and repeat their exact same lines. Weird shit. And it had a beautiful closing and it tied up nicely, all that shit.

"I did that in a way because, well . . . two reasons. One, last year [2000] Screw Puppies [an ensemble made of Annoyance Theater members] was really sloppy and I thought we had a bad presentation of ourselves. Another reason is to demonstrate that as rugged and rough as Annoyance's content is, is that we can still maintain our content and create as beautiful and 'long-form' an experience as anyone can. And that it really isn't the form that's doing it, it's the improvisers that are doing it. You can paint the whore anyway you like, the guy's gonna have a good scene or a bad scene. Good improvisation is good improvisation no matter what form you attach to it. The best form with the worst improvisers, I'm still gonna be fucking reaching for my Game Boy."

Napier continues, "I think structure is very helpful in improvisation as long as that structure is a very helpful guide to improvising. Is it necessary? Obviously not, because the agreed-upon context of structure could be that there is no structure, but even *that* is helpful to improvisers. I can give one good example of great improvisers having a hard time because of no structure, and that is, like at a festival . . . whenever a festival coordinator throws, like, eight great improvisers together, expecting a great, great show, those eight improvisers—before the show starts—have a conversation about 'What are we doing?'

"I've been through about nine of these experiences of 'Let's just not plan anything.' 'Let's just fuck around.' 'No, let's do a Harold, let's do a long form.' 'Why don't we just not think about it at all?' By the time you get on stage, there's ambiguity about what the structure is although the model is that you have six, eight good improvisers. The ambiguity of the agreement of the context of structure causes a disheveled, fucked-up, in-your-head kind of performance often."

One can then ask, is the scene working? Is the relationship heightened? Am I buying what these two people are saying to one another? Am I looking at two people having a relationship or is one person playing with bathroom jokes?

One consistent throughline in interviewing these many personalities during the course of writing the book is that the form is not the thing. The scene's the thing in improvisation, not the form. And certainly not the laugh. There are those who believe one weakness in the approach to long form is the reliance on gimmicks. In discussing *Naked* and its attempts to strip improv to its bare essentials, taking away the "tricks" of improv, there are a few of these fallbacks that long-form improvisers use far too often. The cut-to, the self-reflexive scenes, the inevitable bodily sounds and gross-out humor, the reliance on trite gags that were old in the time of Vaudeville. The answers, according to many of those interviewed, lie in honest, truthful improvisational theatre.

Mick Napier related an exercise in one of his classes. In the exercise, "your goal is to never get a laugh . . . if you do get a laugh, fine, but your goal is to not get a laugh and then I also say that the higher stakes you place in the scene, then the better. . . . If the scene starts, 'Your father passed away,' then play it straight out . . . usually what I get are good, good improvised dramatic scenes with some laughs in them. The laughs have some substantive value and are more organic to the relationship. That's why every day I'm teaching is more refreshing for me. Because the scenes are more involved with the relationship.

"The laughs are more organic, the arc of the scene has greater stakes and, on the other side of it, it's not filled with what I would perceive of as a finite set of conventional improvisational moves and two people are left to just improvise and they have in their minds 'I wanna get laughs.' I feel like I've seen every permutation of that. There's a finite set of characteristics and attributes human beings have when they improvise. But over on the other side, if I eliminate the need to get the laugh, then suddenly they're more intelligent, more emotional, they forget the tactics of the scene, and it's delightful."

Some believe there are those improvisers in Chicago who want to steal the focus on stage and get all the laughs from the audience, because they believe if they get all the laughs, they'll end up in Second City and then on *Saturday Night Live*.

Napier says, "I think as long as *Saturday Night Live* or any other television show uses that kind of talent, those kind of comedy actors, then it's quite normal that people would feel that way. I would look at it this way. What exists that would have them think any other way? Why would they not think about that? What exists that would not have them think about that? To not think about that would be abnormal behavior."

Because of this movement, many attempts at semidramatic improvisation have fallen flat on audiences. As touched upon in looking at Meisner and improv, there are those who believe the theatres and ensembles performing improvisational theatre have not done enough to educate their audiences about the myriad possibilities inherent in their art form. For example, critics reviewing improv shows will sometimes give a show a good review but complain that it was "not funny enough."

Napier says, because of the natural inclination of audiences and critics, to successfully put up a serious improvised show, "I think you really have to plug that concept. 'This improvisational experience is not meant to be funny.' I think you have to declare the context, especially in this city, because the context of improvisation in this city is laugh, laugh, laugh. Whether we like it or not. A show that came close to that, and a show that I really loved was *Naked*. Loved that show! It managed to extend that concept of just improvising for an hour, two people holding onto their scene, the laughs were organic and I think it declared itself as something that didn't have to be funny.

"I really do agree that the venue changes the temper of that performance. When I'm seeing it in a theatre, I have a different expectation as an audience member than I do when I'm in a cabaret. I truly do believe that.

"To digress further, that if you wanted to try a Harold in a theatre, a Harold in a cabaret setting, a long-form Harold kind of thing at Second City, which is a cabaret setting, and then go to Zanies and try to do the same experience where you have the expectation of stand-up and very, very, very, very fast laughs, all of those venues would affect the very same show, wherever it is."

Improv has become such a standard form of entertainment, becoming popular even on television in *Whose Line Is It Anyway?*, that the general public perceives it to contain only the quick-joke format seen on that show.

If many improvisers believe that their work is an art form, then some believe perhaps they need to approach it as an art form and not as a quick leap to television fame. Audience expectations are created by the work gone before. If improvisers wish to change their expectations, then they need to change their work; either that, or they should stop complaining about the perception of their work. People have been socialized to understand music, theatre, and all kinds of forms of artistic expression. Why not do the shows necessary to change the perceptions, to train them on what to expect? It hasn't happened on a large enough scale in Chicago to make any kind of a real impression.

Although improvisers hear what people teach them about good, intelligent scenework in a long form, they do not always apply what they are taught once they face a drunken audience in a smoky cabaret. Those players will meet the audience expectations; their comedy will become sloppy. The best long-form improv groups can play with what they're taught regardless of the audience expectations.

In looking at improvisation as an art form, or whether it's an art form at all, Del Close and Bernie Sahlins' argument about improv as something for which patrons should pay is far from the last argument about improv that we'll see. Whether it is an art form or not, perhaps the greatest justification that improv is an art form is that people argue about it. Chicago is the place to be if you want to talk improv.

# 9     Chicago Improv Now

A nd what is going on now in Chicago?

One important development in the last four years is the emergence of the Chicago Improv Festival, produced by Jonathan Pitts and Frances Callier. Pitts, who had been involved in Chicago improv throughout the 1980s, had in recent years produced Around the Coyote, a performance art festival held every summer in Wicker Park, and Frances Callier had years of experience in Chicago improv, as well as years of experience running the Second City Training Center.

Pitts and Callier had both worked on a children's theatre festival called Magic City, which specialized in teaching children with developmental and physical disabilities the joy of performance. Unfortunately, the festival shut down, and Pitts and Callier ended up having a casual conversation, in which they asked each other why there wasn't yet an improv festival in Chicago. At the time, in 1997, there were two big festivals a year to which many Chicago improv ensembles trekked to perform: Austin and Kansas City. The festivals would feature improv groups from around the country, as well as many instructors for weekend workshops, many of whom came from Chicago. It seemed a little outrageous that Chicago didn't have an improv festival of its own.

Pitts says they decided to put on a festival that "would celebrate Chicago as the epicenter of improv much like Memphis is the epicenter of the blues." He and Callier formulated a nine-month plan to launch the first Chicago Improv Festival in the spring of 1998. Additional one-year, three-year, and five-year plans were drawn up in anticipation of the growth of the festival, something that seemed assured given the environment in which the festival was to exist. Chicago already had an audience base for improv. Both festivals in Austin and Kansas City have since faltered due to terrible financial problems, due in part to the fact that the audience for these kinds of festivals simply doesn't exist in the host cities.

For the first Chicago festival, ensembles were invited from around the country, the performances taking place at the Annoyance Theater and ImprovOlympic. After four improv festivals, Pitts and Callier are planning five different venues for the fifth annual festival in the spring of 2002. The first stage is the Mainstage, where the headliners like Upright Citizens Brigade, Baby Wants Candy, and other heavy hitters perform. Many alumni of Chicago improv who are now with *Saturday Night Live, Mad TV,* and *Late Night with Conan O'Brien* come into town to perform on the Chicago Improv Festival Mainstage, which receives much of the focus of the press. For the last two years, the CIF mainstage was at the nine hundred-seat Athenaeum Theatre on the North Side of Chicago.

The Showcase venue takes place at a second, smaller location (2001 saw the Showcase take place at the Playground, a ninety-seat venue) that specializes in more local talent. Some nights the Showcase will have a theme. One performance featured nothing but solo improvisers. Improv 'Til Dawn is exactly as its title would suggest, a mass multitude of improv groups, each of whom is given a fifteen-minute slot in an all-night show that goes 'til . . . well, dawn.

In an ambitious move, the 2002 festival will feature two more stages. The first of the new stages is a Fringe stage, which will feature more experimental improv that, according to Pitts, "doesn't have to be funny." The fifth stage will be a Sketch stage, which Pitts hopes will help define the difference between sketch comedy and pure improvised performance by giving the sketch comedy practitioners their own venue.

For a festival that Pitts says many people didn't think would succeed, simply based on the fact that Chicago had done just fine without a festival for forty years, the CIF's growth has mirrored in an accelerated way the growth of Chicago improv itself. From two stages to five stages in five years is an astonishing accomplishment. What's more amazing is that there's enough talent to fill those stages over the course of a six-day festival.

Outside of those six days, in Chicago there's an improv-festival atmosphere almost every day of the year. Every week there are a few dozen improv groups performing at ImprovOlympic and the Playground and many more performing at bars around the city. The range of talent you'll see in Chicago on any given night will range from brilliant, insightful, and truly hysterical to embarrassing and pathetic.

Today, in Chicago, in the year 2002, the cynic can say that improv isn't really theatre, nor is it a philosophy or a way of life. It is merely an *industry,* say some, and improvisers have a trade-school mentality about their experiences here and follow the exact steps they feel will get them onto a Second City stage. If one is to follow the cynical rationale that improv is merely an industry, then the John Rockefeller of improv is the Second City. Boasting two resident stages in Chicago and resident stages in Las Vegas, Toronto, Cleveland, and Detroit, a highly profitable business communications division, multiple touring companies, and a training center that teaches workshops to a thousand eager-to-learn improvisers in Chicago alone, Second City is best described as the top of the heap of Chicago improv.

While ComedySportz pays their performers a small stipend for performing, Second City is the only improvisationally based theatre in Chicago that can pay their resident performers living wages. Even touring company members get paid, but it's really the lucky ones on the Mainstage and e.t.c. who get to pay rent with their checks from Second City.

Thus, the theatre has the distinct advantage of being able to raid talent at will from the other theatres and workshops in Chicago. Actors from around the world flock to Chicago with the hope of being one of the twelve people in the city who have a regular gig on the Mainstage or the e.t.c. stage.

Besides ImprovOlympic and the Second City, the theatres that produce improvisationally based theatre include Annoyance Productions, WNEP Theater, ComedySportz Chicago, the Playground Theater, Noble Fool Theater, Free Associates, and many smaller improv groups that exist independently of any of the brick-and-mortar theatres, traveling the city and performing in bars and nightclubs to attempt to get the kind of exposure they need to make the trek to *Saturday Night Live*. Why so many theatres?

First of all, those hundreds and hundreds of new improvisers that the Second City Training Center and ImprovOlympic churn out love the work they're doing so much they want to continue it and there's simply no room for the two theatres to accommodate everyone. After all, they need to dispose of the old students somehow in order to bring new ones in.

Chicago is a far easier city in which to start a theatre than New York. Rent in Chicago, while seeming awfully high if you're coming from a rural area with a low cost of living, is several times less expensive than the cost of maintaining a theatre in Manhattan. Also, Chicago is a generally welcoming city to new theatres. A theatre company can rent a storefront business and convert it into a small black box with relatively little cost. Chicago, like every city, has complicated laws regarding entertainment licenses and liquor licenses, but it is far more feasible for the enterprising group of actors to build a theatre in Chicago than in any of the other major metropolitan theatrical centers.

Improv theatres also have extra advantages that other theatres in Chicago do not have. First of all, improv theatres don't have to worry about production costs. In improv, the performers practice object work and create their own environments and imagine themselves wearing costumes, so improv theatres don't have to worry about maintaining a budget for building sets, renting costumes, or finding that early twentieth-century phone that's crucial to the play they happen to be putting up.

The traditional Second City stage consists of a couple of chairs and whatever condition the stage is in. In recent revues, Second City has redesigned their stage in an attempt to work with the thematic thrust of the revue and it has been a successful venture. But Second City, of course, has the money. For places like ImprovOlympic and the Playground, where every show is completely improvised, there's no reason to change the stage.

Another financial advantage of starting up an improv theatre is you don't pay your performers. Not getting paid is sort of a fact of life anyway throughout Chicago theatre. Getting more stage time than in any other city in the world is sufficient enough. Plus, when Screen Actors Guild members have an unemployment rate hovering somewhere around 95 percent, actors learn that not getting paid is a simple fact of life in their profession.

Improv theatres survive. The current Noble Fool Theater, the first improvisationally based theatre *ever* in the downtown Loop Theater District, rose from the ashes of the Improv Institute, which had shows from 1984 to 1994. It is a theatre that is long forgotten by improvisers today, but for a Chicago theatre, a ten-year existence is an eternity.

The desire of many improvisers is to get onto *Saturday Night Live*. How do they think they can get there? By getting hired by Second City, of course!

The intense competitiveness to get attention and get one of those twelve resident spots at Second City can have negative impact on performances. In an effort to get laughs, an individual on an improv group can ruin a show in his or her drive to be the one to be "noticed."

There really is no way to avoid this kind of destructive behavior but you can be sure you work with people who simply want to do good work, which is more than possible in Chicago. You merely have to accept that the boundless ambition exists and attempt to align yourself with people who just want to be great at what they do. The long-form improvisers who have gone on to success writing and performing for television have those jobs based on their merits and not how much of a stand-up comic they can pretend to be or how many jokes they could tell on stage. The reason that so many people from Jazz Freddy and the Family have become successful is because they were great *ensembles*.

To have the opportunity to show your stuff, to get on stage, is the real prize in Chicago, worth more than any measly paycheck you could receive. Some improvisers put themselves on multiple improv groups at multiple theatres at the same time, with the hope that by multiplying their stage time exponentially, they are more likely to be seen by someone and handed a big wad of cash to appear on television. The other thought is that the more stage time they get, the better they get. This is logical enough.

Some improvisers may have a schedule looking something like this (please note team names are completely imaginary):

Sundays 12–3 Second City improv class

Sundays 4–7 Rehearsal with IO team Plastic Southern People

Sundays 7–10 Meisner class at WNEP Theater

Mondays 7–10 IO class—Level Five

Tuesdays 7–10 Second City sketch-writing class

Wednesdays 7–10 Rehearsal with Playground ensemble The Fish Can Really See Me

Some people see this as a problem. Noah Gregoropoulos had the experience of being on Jazz Freddy, a group so committed to that group and that group alone, they rehearsed at least four times a week. He was asked which is better, rehearsing with one group nine times a week or nine groups each once a week.

He answered, "That's not an easy answer, because it really depends on how good they are, and also depends on what level they're at.

"Are we talking about a student? You can spend nine days a week wasting time on rehearsals for one show with a namby-pamby director, a cast that are friends rather than the best people available, and a show that is uninspired and has no vision. And your time can be much better spent at the buffet line trying everything."

Traditionally, improv classes take place once a week and improv group (team) rehearsals take place once a week, so one is able to pack his week with classes with multiple training centers and rehearsals with multiple groups. This assists with exposure, schmoozing, etc.

This culture of "being seen" is often seen as the norm for Chicago improvisers. Some will do everything they can to get as much stage time as possible. Multiple experiences are important. Still, if an improviser who rehearses with four groups a week instead rehearses four times a week with one group, building an impenetrable group mind, who knows what kind of heights she can reach?

The argument exists that Chicago improv has gotten too vast for any one group to make an impact like Jazz Freddy and the Family did. A group like Sheila from Hyde Park in Chicago doesn't fit into the Second City/ImprovOlympic niche of Chicago improv and thus is not as well known as other groups that have direct relationships with those institutions.

Despite the feeling that there are "big, important" theatres in improv (Second City, ImprovOlympic, ComedySportz), there is still the rebellious feeling of outsiders. Some people believe improvisational theatre still receives little or no respect from the broader Chicago theatre landscape, mostly because the market is so completely saturated that the majority of improvised shows in the city are completely unwatchable. If a critic sees two or three awful improv shows in a row, he will likely live with the prejudice that improv is awful.

Unfortunately, Spolin's credo that "everyone can improvise" is sorely tested every evening, according to Rob Mello, who says, "Sure, everyone can improvise. Everyone can paint, too, but that doesn't mean someone's going to buy their painting."

The multitude of training centers in Chicago gives a few students the false impression that if they have the money to take an improv class, then they're ready to take the stage as a full-fledged improvisational actor. A bar will be eager to let an improv group perform sans rent on a Wednesday night if it can sell drinks to the audience members. It happens all over the city. Unlike with a band, the bar almost never pays any fee whatsoever to an improv group.

So you have your ultimate no-budget stage show. No rent to pay, no actors to pay, no set to build . . . it's all free of cost. The only fear you have is not bringing enough audience members to the show and giving the bar owner reason to kick you out and pull in something that he or she thinks will bring in more patrons.

In a worst-case scenario, in order to keep their place in a bar, the improv group will make sure they invite all their friends and coworkers to the show to support them. Inevitably, the reaction to the show is much stronger than if there were an audience full of strangers. The performers believe the laughter of their friends is a sometimes false indication of the quality of their work when it's often just poor to average. The performers then lose the focus of improving themselves through the strengthening of the group mind.

One of the more recent developments in Chicago improv is that many of the new improvisers who are coming into the city are ambitious young men coming right out of college, what one director said were annoying "frat boys."

Noah Gregoropoulos says, "The entire current generation of young male improvisers is basically a pet peeve of mine. I would say nine out of ten students who walk into the IO are doing an imitation somewhere in the spectrum in between Chris Farley and Matthew Perry rather than having anything of their own." This, according to Gregoropoulos, is more of a project than a real problem.

For those who complain about the politics of the Chicago improv community, there are those who believe there are politics once you have more than one person in a room in any given situation. It's all part of the makeup of a society. Everyone wants to make the big time. Some people are fairly obnoxious and rather poor at it. Parties and bars like the Old Town Ale House are the centers of improv networking. Plus, now in the modern age, there are dozens of websites devoted to improv, many of which originate just from Chicago. Message boards allow improvisers from around the world to discuss their work, or at least trade bits, trying to impress each other with their rapier wit.

There is a little fear along with the comedy. With so few legitimate paying jobs in Chicago improv, the power is believed to be held in very few hands. But, what a lot of improvisers don't realize is that they are probably making more in their day jobs than the "power brokers" are making running improv theatres or teaching or performing or doing a combination of all three.

Now, let's not say that the Chicago improv culture is all negative. Quite simply, you will meet some of the best friends you ever had in the world! There is a camaraderie that develops unlike any other you will experience or have experienced in high school or college. Some people will become family.

You will struggle with your classmates and fellow ensemble members. You will watch them grow into better performers just as you grow into a better performer. If you don't reach the heights of fame, you can always say you "knew them when." Few things are more exciting than seeing your friends succeed.

The memories you keep will last forever. The best scenes you ever did, looking back and realizing how awful you used to be . . . all valuable life experiences.

You can see such a wide variety of comedic styles in Chicago that you can see nowhere else. Many improvisers from around the country make a weekend trek to the city in an attempt to see as many shows at as many theatres as possible in an effort to decide whether they should relocate there. Sometimes a weekend is enough to really get a feel for the improv community if one takes in shows at three or so of the improv theatres. Often, out-of-towners end up coming for the Chicago Improv Festival and decide they should stay here.

Moving to Chicago is an adventure for many. In terms of making a living in Chicago as a potential member of the entertainment industry, people like Mick Napier of Annoyance Productions are attempting to make Chicago more of a production center for film and television. There are mighty obstacles in place. New York and Los Angeles have a pretty firm grip on showbiz, but there are still more opportunities for the actor in Chicago.

Beyond the world of improvisational theatre, there are dozens of theatre companies performing the works of playwrights old and new. Plenty of commercial work is done. There's more than enough in Chicago to give the actor the ropes, going through the pains of auditioning for the hundreds of plays put up every year.

There is no single better place to study improvisation in the world. Places like the UCB Theater in New York and IO West in Los Angeles have taken up the work of Chicago improv on the coasts, but when it comes to the variety of improv styles and the theatres at one's disposal, there is no better place than Chicago.

# 10 Choosing Your Direction

Once you arrive in Chicago, find your apartment and perhaps even a job, you set off on your dream to become a master in the home of improv. Now it's time to take some classes! You've read all about Chicago improv, some of the things that have occurred in the last twenty years or so. And this doesn't even cover the beginning. For example, Rich Talarico, Stephnie Weir, and Bob Dassie turned ImprovOlympic on its ear recently with a jazz-inspired improvisational show called *Trio,* which ran Sunday nights at 11:15 to accommodate Weir and Talarico's Second City schedules. It proved the glories of a small ensemble and how the right talented people can thrive in such an environment. Since shows like *Trio, Sybil,* and *Naked* have been successful with one or two people improvising, many other performers in Chicago have chosen to stretch themselves in this manner.

In fact, the best shows at IO now run at that time because loyal alumni who now perform at Second City love to come back and perform on the old stage. It's hell for someone who wants to get some sleep for the workweek, but the quality of work being performed in that time slot makes the bleary eyes on Monday morning worth it.

Other great forms and shows are being performed every week. You can usually keep track on the Internet and at the theatres themselves. There's almost always a buzz of some kind in this town.

But how to create your own buzz? You've heard all this stuff about Chicago improv and all the wonderful opportunities here to perform and you've soaked up these ideas about Meisner and the Hero's Journey and you've read Sweet's book and *Truth in Comedy* and you decide that Chicago is the place to go to reach artistic self-actualization. What do you do once you get here?

There are nearly two thousand students of improvisation in Chicago at any given moment, taking classes at one of the myriad of specialized training centers or else at one of Chicago's many theatre training centers (like Center Theater and Act One) or at one of the city's colleges or universities. There is no richer tapestry of theatre in the world. One may argue that New York's quilt of performance features a greater variety of colors, but Chicago has the upper hand when it comes to the number of legitimate, realistic opportunities to get stage time.

This includes improv. Second City, ImprovOlympic, and other training centers stress the importance of performing in front of a live audience to augment your learning experience. Even if you have experience with improv in whichever town from which you have come, there's nothing remotely like the Chicago experience. We're going to cover several of the best places to take classes in Chicago: ImprovOlympic, the Second City Training Center, the Annoyance, and the Playground. There are plenty of other places where one can take improv classes, including WNEP Theater, Comedy-Sportz, and the granddaddy of them all, Players Workshop. The various locations of these training centers are included in Appendix 2, which can be easily found near the back cover of this book.

If you think you know the Harold because you read *Truth in Comedy*, there's nothing like learning it in person at the theatre where it was born. As many books as there are on methods of theatrical performance, there's nothing quite like experiencing it from the masters.

## ImprovOlympic (IO)

ImprovOlympic is the natural starting point for our discussion on training centers. Although it hasn't been around as long as Second City, IO has had a formal training program for longer than Second City and the classes really have formed the basis for just about everything that has popped up in Chicago improv for the past twenty years.

Since the passing of Del Close in 1999, and Charna Halpern concentrating on producing both the IO in Chicago and IO West in Los Angeles, the duties of running the training center have fallen to other hands.

Liz Allen has been the training center director of IO since 2000. She began her improv training in 1991 at Second City, and one of her teachers recommended ImprovOlympic and she and several of her fellow students called up Charna Halpern and started to take classes at the training center of the ImprovOlympic the following year. One thing Allen remembers most about being introduced to the culture there was that "whoever's in your Level One [class]—you'll be friends for life."

Originally, because the size of the training center was more manageable, students were able to get into Harold teams much more quickly. "At that point ImprovOlympic only had three levels, so by the middle of Level Two, our class had split into two teams, the Lost Yetis and Frank Booth (originally called Mr. Pink). I wasn't originally on Frank Booth but they added me later and we were together for four years.

"In about 1997 I started coaching Valhalla [a Harold team] and I coached them for three-and-a-half years and then I quit coaching them, but before that I had started coaching Mission Improvable, so I've been coaching consecutively for six years. I've been teaching at ImprovOlympic for easily four years and then two years ago I won Coach of the Year at the Del Close Awards and won last year also. So I'm the two-year reigning title holder of Coach of the Year, so all that led to myself being sort of a natural pick when Jason Chin was ready to stop being the director and Charna asked if I would be interested in taking that position.

"Almost ten months now I've been the training center director. . . . I'm lucky that the content of the classes had been hammered out pretty thoroughly by the time I took over because we shifted to five levels a long time ago and I think we also have a really long history of teachers. All of our teachers in the training center have been teaching for a minimum of two years."

Allen explains, "The curriculum was already decided. We have four Level One classes, four Level Two classes. Then we have some attrition, so then we go down to three Level Three, three Level Four, three Level Five, and then you get into your performance class. We just recently started breaking that into two groups, so then when they do their show, they'll probably each get an act and then two acts, so that was my own idea to break up and use the space more efficiently; but I feel very confident and comfortable with what's taught in each level and there's actually some thought and some method to the madness. It's like algebra. I always tell people when they say, 'Why can't I just go into Level Two? I finished Second City,' it's because the whole theory of total true improvisational long form that we teach builds it on each previous class.

"In Level One, we want to give them the introduction to the Harold. I mean, we throw it at them in piecemeal fashion, but the whole point of people coming to ImprovOlympic is to learn to do Harold, which is the signature piece. So they're coming into Level One, we let them know what it's like. Then we give them some very definite tools about trusting and playing as a team and learning to be free, to create together. Because these are group artists, it's not a singular art form like painting or stand-up or something like that. It's a group art. So we introduce people to the concept of group work. We have, you know, your standard improv games, but we also get into scenes, and techniques of scenes and how to play it real. And how to not be funny and how to—We really start introducing them to a lot of Del's theories that the best long-form improvisers are the people that reflect life and don't try to come up with funny situations, that truth is always funnier than life. We want people to learn how to be honest on stage, to learn how to show themselves. In Level One, we just hope to accomplish that people will feel comfortable being themselves, trusting the group, and will have a strong idea of what Harold is, and also some very definite stylized games and scenic techniques.

"And then in Level Two, we just go deeper with all of the above, particularly scene ideas, ways to learn to play characters in scenes and more of beginning to link the idea of games and scenes and games and scenes, because that's what a piece of long form is. There's a lot of standard exercises, and Paul Grondy is usually the Level Two teacher.

"Level Two also delves deeper into the idea of what makes improv scenes more interesting to watch than not. And at that point, too, in Level Two, people are getting a little bit more confident and they've figured out what some of their fears are and we start to address that.

"And then Level Three, which is the level I teach, is the big-giant-group-work level. It's all about connecting as the group and this is the part where I really sort of pay homage to Del because I took his class three times because it was so powerful about his idea that human beings don't interact as a group anymore. And that improvisation is an opportunity for us to give to the other person and work as a greater whole than as an individual.

"That's the level I teach, and so does Susan Messing, and we begin to look at bringing character in and environment and going outside of yourself for inspiration in scenes. Like, pick up anything and play someone from your life and if you change your physicality, emotion will follow.

"Then in Level Four, it's like our hardcore scenework class. At that point people are ready for a lot harder critiquing and we raise the bar on their level of performance and we also kind of have taken a break from scenework from Level Two up until Four so it's good . . . because they back into Four almost refreshed.

"Then we start doing Harolds. A lot of Harolds. So that they learn how to maneuver and navigate a long form. We all believe that in order to develop and play in lots of different forms, you gotta learn one, and I don't think there's any better place to start than the Harold.

"And then [in Level] Five they create their own long forms and they learn to play with and manipulate long forms. They learn to see patterns in work and they learn the idea of callbacks. They learn how if you start separately your worlds will absolutely unite if you're connected as a group. So they sort of get the big payoff of all they've been building for by creating their own work. Then in the performance-level class, they create their own form and then actually have it as a show at the theatre for—the length of the runs vary, from four to eight weeks, depending on the schedule at the theatre—and then they can invite all their friends and family and that's when they work with Noah."

"Noah" is Noah Gregoropoulos. He has the unenviable task of following Del Close's footsteps in teaching the "top" level at ImprovOlympic. In teaching the performance class—or as some would call it, an extension of "Five" or even "Five B"—Gregoropoulos takes a simple approach.

"In terms of class, to be very honest with you, I don't look to have brilliant formal innovation in a class," says Gregoropoulos. "A fifth-level class, you're basically working with a range of competence level and I don't think it's fair to do, to have a Level Five B class or performance-level class doing Close Quarters, something it took the best improvisers in Chicago eight months to perfect.

"To me, there's a couple of functions of a Level Five B show. One is, I want the people who aren't performing yet anywhere to have a performance experience that doesn't suck wind. I mean, that makes them look reasonably good, because it's kind of . . . I feel like it's their *last chance to get on a team,* or whatever, and for a lot of people, it works, you know, because it's like they just for some reason slipped through the cracks. There's some pretty decent people. They're competent to better-than-average but aren't blowing anyone's doors off but could probably, you know, spend a couple of schedules on a team and benefit from that.

"I would like those people to have an opportunity to be seen in something where they can look at least competent," says Gregoropoulos. "Once in a while you'll have a class . . . basically, [the team] People of Earth for the most part were a class . . . with a couple of other people that were generally pretty good and they did a pretty sophisticated form for their Five B that I wouldn't throw at any class. For one thing, it was a class of eleven people. I usually have about thirty-some students going at a time now, not in the same class, but still, two classes of sixteen to eighteen people . . . it's gonna have a lot of Harold qualities to it, stuff they've already worked on in the program, with some innovative editing, moves, or . . . some classes it's more the source of the improvisation is what comes to them. Like the team Clef Pallete would improvise to music and literature. And that wasn't something you always see, or rather than taking a suggestion, someone would be assigned to being in some recorded music and they'd improvise to the recorded music and then all of a sudden that would be the source of the scene or someone would actually read to them from Proust or whatever and they would respond to that, so basically using the techniques of Harold and Deconstruction because, basically, it doesn't take forty weeks to really learn Harold and Deconstruction well, it takes years. And those are the things they've kind of been working on."

Liz Allen also explains that Charna Halpern still makes sure she comes in contact with all the students. Allen says, "Yeah, Charna likes to meet everyone in Level One and she signs everyone up so that she introduces herself to all the students. T. J. Jagadowski is our other main Level One teacher. And we also have some electives at the theatre, we have the standard elective now of Long-Form Techniques."

In order to take the standard elective or any other elective, Allen says, "We like that you've already performed or at least are going to Level Three to take our elective, and other electives have other requirements, but right now we're trying to have a standard Long-Form Techniques elective."

When asked what sets ImprovOlympic's training center apart from the myriad of other training centers out there, Allen says it's "our incredible longevity of teaching staff and the dedication and the loyalty of the teachers. They continue to teach, love to teach, take very few breaks . . . and also . . . frankly, I'll just be blunt . . . I don't think there's a bad teacher in our lot. I'm not just saying that because I'm the training center director. First, here's what we do to hire a teacher: They had to have coached [a Harold team] for a while, like six months to a year. Then they have to have substituted for another teacher, and then the first class they get, we absolutely get evaluations on them, and we review what the students say about them. Charna really doesn't want to just throw somebody up there who's performed, you know, around the country and colleges, so I think that's what sets us apart, really, is the quality of teachers.

"The other thing that sets us apart at ImprovOlympic is that— and the reason I kind of took this job is, I thought, 'What would it be like if people were really nurtured while they learned to improvise?' Because I would have really loved that. I mean, even though I had wonderful teachers, like I feel very blessed, like you said, a lot of those teachers I had and Norm Holly, but like Martin [de Maat], and Michael Gellman who's still there [at Second City]—he's great too. And Del here.

"But I also think I was thrown to the dogs a wee, teeny bit. And just like, a sink-or-swim sort of thing, so even though I don't think I come into every class and hold people's hands, I really try to listen and when I hear a complaint from a student or a student gives me a comment, we make adjustments. We had some complaints that our classes were getting kind of big in one level last session, so I split them in two.

"We're growing so much. I can't believe how much. I mean, improv in general has grown since we got involved, I mean, isn't it amazing?

"We're trying to keep the small feel of IO but let it grow. Here's the one thing, that was the one reason to keep all the classes in one space, because obviously the next move is going to be a bigger space; we need, like, a college compound, IO. If IO had a college compound, that would be great.

"[Charna] doesn't want to bring people in just to bring people in. We always have a waiting list. For example, classes started this week, we already have fifty on our waiting list for June. If we had the space, we could have more classes right now, but it's always that balance of, how do we make it personal? If we had more performance space, I bet you we'd have more classes."

## The Playground

The Playground offers opportunities for improvisers on two levels. Beginning in the year 2000, the young improv co-op ran a program of workshops they called the Master's Series.

They call these Master's Series "advanced workshops for working improvisers." An instructor will take a single specific skill area in improvisation and teach a single, three-hour workshop covering that skill area. The series usually lasts four weeks, with four different instructors each teaching one of these single-day workshops. The teachers themselves come up with the subjects of their workshops.

The classes are intended to increase specific skills in improvisers who have already completed all the levels at ImprovOlympic,

Second City and Annoyance and who are currently performing. Realizing that these theatres had made their livings for over a decade in building up huge improv training centers, the Playground found a niche in these specialized workshops, that usually—as of this date in 2001—run about forty dollars each.

Some examples of workshops taught in the Master's Series follow:

### If You Got It, Flaunt It! or Physical Education 101—Jack McBrayer

Tired of doing two-person talking-head scenes? Use your body to its fullest potential to physicalize your scenework! Investigate the possibilities of physical comedy in ways you thought only Bob Dassie could achieve. Object work, environment, non-verbal scenework, and physicality of character will be explored.

### Make Your Long Form Matter—Liz Allen

Learn to discover unexpected connections in the later portions of your long form. By utilizing callbacks, scene revisitations, and other techniques, you will learn to discover the links that naturally appear. Trust and watch as different worlds merge gracefully, realistically, and hilariously in your pieces.

### Finding Order in Long Form Chaos—Joe Bill

Long form improvisation is not just a series of unrelated scenes. Learn to make connections and stitch together fragments within a piece to create meaning out of pandemonium.

The other opportunity for improvisers at the Playground is the Incubator program. The theatre was founded on the basis that independent improv ensembles would perform at the Playground as self-governing entities. However, the issue soon came up that perhaps not everyone was already with an improv group.

So the theatre began the Incubator program with the intention of assisting in the building of new improv ensembles. There are bimonthly auditions in which performers are split into groups of about eight or nine people and then are asked to do individual scenes and then a long form. The auditions usually bring out about seventy people, out of which there are two ensembles formed and then assigned a coach. Weekly rehearsals ensue, about four or six before the Incubator ensembles get their own Tuesday-night show, sort of a comfort zone for the first two shows where they can invite friends and not feel the pressure of performing at a regular Playground show.

Then they have a run of shows on Thursday nights, and then they "graduate" the Incubator program. The ensembles are no longer guaranteed stage time at the Playground but usually get some more. The coaches of these groups attempt to foster the idea of self-governing artistic expression in these new ensembles and sometimes the groups become full-fledged member ensembles, becoming an official part of the co-op. Not so much a formal class as a way to learn how to be in an improv group, the Incubator program has enjoyed success and attracts many hopeful auditioners.

Several of the Incubator ensembles have gone on to become member ensembles as well.

## Annoyance Productions

According to founder Mick Napier, the Annoyance's training program can best be summed up in two words: Fuck it. There are three tiers of classes, but so concerned was the Annoyance in avoiding any sense of hierarchy in their system, they ceased labeling their classes as "Level One, Two, Three" and elected to name their classes after animals. However, there still is a certain order in which you need to take the classes. The Lemur classes come first, taught by Rebecca Sohn and Mark Sutton; the class known as Vulture is taught by Joe Bill, and Okapi by Mick Napier. The description for Okapi says that "it focuses exclusively on personal attention with special emphasis on initiating scenes and sustaining the energy and commitment of characters within scenes. You must have completed the Lemur and Vulture classes to take this class."

Mick Napier answered this when posed with a question: "Why take classes at Annoyance? My answer is always a question: What do you want to do? What do you want? If you want stage time, if that's really important, then ImprovOlympic will offer you that. If you want to learn more about sketch comedy, maybe Second City will teach you more about that. If you want to learn how to improvise a scene and learn more about *your* improvisation and what's holding you up and what is making you good, I can't imagine anything better than the Annoyance for that."

Annoyance classes eschew the usual three-hour class format. Napier says, "I teach on Saturdays from noon to 2 as I've done for about *sixty-two years.* Every week, 12 to 2. I only teach two hours because I found that when I taught three hours at Second City is that I didn't have enough . . . I was quite bored trying to fill that time. A lot of my teaching is in reaction to the way I've been taught. I have listened to teachers talk for an hour and a half more times than I care to admit in classes I've taken.

"It's very important for me to have my students up a lot. Improvising a lot. And I found that if I do that, I eliminate my bullshit talking, that really two hours is a sufficient amount of time to get across a point or two about improvisation.

"I let them go their course. What I'll do sometimes is put a time limit on it, we're going to improvise one-minute scenes, so that I know that in or out of a minute, I can call that scene out. If I do interrupt a scene, then I declare the context of that usually: 'I am going to be interrupting scenes.' I do a thing that is . . . it's basically, I say to them, 'Your goal is to improvise and keep the scene going and my goal is to stop you any way I can with any little thing I see that's fucking the scene up, either personally or scenically, improvisationally.' So I do that and I will say, 'Go,' and then someone will take a breath on a scene and just read something on that scene. Some dumb thing, but that's the context generally—I don't side coach or interrupt scenes.

"It is, improvisation, is in my opinion, that concept is attached to the first three seconds of improvisations, where, just letting your head snap and go, 'Fuck it!' Do anything, just do something, get out of your head. . . ."

The Annoyance also doesn't spend a lot of time concentrating on the basic rules of improv, making it a training program that is not necessarily well suited to be an improv student's very first course. "One thing I don't do with improvisation, when I see an improv scene, the way I look at an improv scene, I can't think of one thing that has been regarded as a conventional rule of improvisation that I look for, I don't even actively ignore them anymore. It doesn't occur to me. So when I see an improv scene, the entire scene could be filled with questions and the word *no* and my mind, the way it is right now, doesn't even register that there are a lot of questions in the scene."

## The Second City Training Center

We all know Second City. But how about their training program? Formalized in 1986 as one of the first major moves Andrew Alexander made after he bought the theatre, the training program was split into two different programs for a number of years and in the past five years has recently expanded into one of the biggest actor training centers (non-university) in the nation. They boast training not only in the cities where there exists a Second City theatre (Chicago, Detroit, Cleveland, Toronto, Las Vegas) but also in Los Angeles and New York.

Rob Chambers has been the director of the Chicago training center for two years. "I was previously a freelance director. I came to Chicago ten years ago, took the graduate program at DePaul and had been directing shows in New York and Chicago when a few years ago, I became marketing manager at the League of Chicago Theaters." That experience in theatre administration helped Chambers enter the hallowed halls of the Second City empire.

"I was in the nonprofit theatre for years and I really wanted to work in the commercial theatre and see the difference. When I first came up here, I was like, 'This is the biggest acting training center in the world!'" In any given eight-week term, there are between eight hundred and one thousand students enrolled in the Chicago training center alone.

The training center's two primary programs are the Beginner's program and the Conservatory program. The Beginner's program consists of five levels of classes, each meeting three hours a week (all training center classes follow this model) for eight weeks. The levels are labeled A to E and, according to Chamber, are for anybody with little or no improv experience or stage experience.

"It attracts people from all walks of life. Definitely some people use it as an acting tool, but don't forget Spolin started this work for kids and in social work. Some people take the classes because it increases business skills, or because it makes you more confident in front of people. People might be latent performers, people in their late twenties and early thirties who have been in the business world for ten years are investigating the performing bug.

"There are people who take classes because they need to have a good time. I remember an oncology nurse who's taking classes. She told me, 'It's really great not to think about death for three hours a week.'

"Ad agencies send people with their creative teams for team building. Yes-anding is not a concept that's taught in the business sector."

For those students who have finished Level E or else have had at least a year of traditional acting experience beyond high school and at least some improv proficiency, there is the Conservatory program. Rob Chambers explains, "The initial purpose of the Conservatory program was to prepare performers for Second City stages. That is, to learn improvisation as Bernie Sahlins defined it, as a process for writing a sketch comedy revue."

The levels are assigned by numbers rather than letters in the Conservatory program, and potential students need to audition for Level One. The auditions are what one might expect in an improv environment, concentrating on proficiency in scenes and games, treating them as collaborative rather than as stand-up comedy. Then, the students go through the eight-week three-hours-per-class routine in Level One and Level One A, at which point they go through another round of auditions to get into Level Two.

"In the first few levels, we make sure everyone is speaking the same language improvisationally," says Chambers. The auditions for Level Two are to make sure everyone is speaking that same language. Levels Two and Three continue the study of improvisation, delving deeper into different styles and content, considering that Second City's heritage is steeped in a tradition of political and social satire. Levels Four and Five then continue the evolution of the students, showing how an ensemble uses improvised scenes and transforms them into a written show.

Chambers says, "So that by the end, the students know what it's like to produce a Second City show. Marketing their Level Five show is important because often the Level Five classes go on to produce their own shows. To which we say, the more the merrier! It's building an audience, an awareness for the art form."

What Chambers calls "Improvisation for Actors" is a class more leaned toward improvisation as product rather than just the traditional process like Second City has used it for years. Chambers says of the students, "Some might be working actors who use it as a workout. The class is more of improvisation as performance, developing a one-act play as improv. First couple of levels are really an actor's workout and then developing the play."

The class is very popular among professional actors. Chambers recalls, "When *Ragtime* and *Show Boat* were in Chicago for extended runs, many of the actors took these classes to grease their wheels. In Vegas, cast members from Blue Man Group and Cirque du Soleil are taking it."

They also have a traditional acting scene study class, as well as a high school–level improv class. That class originated in many ways because of the demand for talent at that age. "There is such a demand from casting directors for high school–aged actors. Sixteen to twenty is really hot," says Chambers.

Out of all of the courses Second City teaches, "Comedy Writing class has seen the biggest growth," according to Chambers.

"It originally developed as a way to help Conservatory students. When we reach Level Four and Five, we expect students to be familiar with various styles of comedy sketch writing. It fills a gap in case they aren't familiar with these.

"The surprising thing is the number of students who have no intention of performing. They want to learn how to write and to write comically. People who always wanted to write."

Like the Conservatory program, the Comedy Writing program goes on for five levels. In Level Five, they write and produce their own sketch comedy revue, cast it from training center students, and have their own three-week run.

"We've placed so many people in the comedy writing field," says Chambers. "We've found people that that's what they want to do . . . with people like Tina Fey becoming successes as writers."

Because of the vast growth of the training center, classes have had to go outside the realm of Second City property. For example, for the past two years, all beginning classes have been held at the local St. Alphonsus School.

But recently, Second City has taken a lease on the fourth-floor space at Piper's Alley (which houses the Second City e.t.c., a restaurant, Starbucks, and multiscreen movie theatres, all next door to the main Second City theatre), just left of Donny's Skybox Theater. A series of studios will function as the whole training center. All classes will be under one roof. The new training center facilities are expected to be open by the time this book hits the shelves.

They also have classes at the Metropolis Performing Arts Center in Arlington Heights, a Northwest suburb of Chicago, for those of you unfortunate enough to move to the suburbs.

Chambers says, "We recently had a regional training center meeting. The challenge we face is a sense of a consistent curriculum, although we need flexibility in each market. The actor in New York is very different from the actor in Chicago. With Marty gone, we're going through a transition period." Martin de Maat, the longtime artistic director of the Second City Training Center and one of the most beloved teachers in Chicago, passed away in early 2001.

"I've named four different program heads," says Chambers, "and the artistic director of the program is chosen between one of the four people every year."

Beginning and high school: Anne Libera (currently artistic director)

Conservatory: Norm Holly

Improvisation for Actors: Michael Gellman

Writing: Kim Clarke

Chambers enthuses about the cooperative atmosphere that exists in Chicago. "We say [after taking classes at Second City], 'Go to IO, go to the Annoyance.' Everyone's going to glean everything they can from everyone's styles and build their own. That's what's exciting about Chicago."

In continuing to expand the Second City Training Center, the improvisational theatre that became an immediate success in 1959 and has become something like an empire in its fifth decade, the organization hopes to prepare its students to become the best new talent on their stage. If they do well and can garner attention from teachers, who often are also directors of the Touring Company, auditions may become successful and performers can be hired by the Touring Company (called TourCo for short).

It is important, however, to distinguish that the training center is not "the answer" if one wishes to be hired by Second City. You have to be really good, too. Even if you are hired by the Touring Company, you end up performing *The Best of Second City*, which consists of the best scenes written for revues over the past forty years. New scenes are incorporated at times, but the majority of scenes are old ones (but great ones!). An improvised set will often follow the performance, which is the best time one can flex one's muscles on stage.

Then, as mentioned before, there are only a handful of positions available on the resident stages. And sometimes they hire people who weren't even in the Touring Company for those positions. In an enormously competitive environment, it is important to consider that the best thing to do for yourself is simply learn and grow as a person and a performer and not worry where you're going. After all, one of the true beauties of improv is to learn to live in the moment.

So come to Chicago! There's plenty of room. And if you don't think there's room for you, you can always make room. Plenty before you have done so with great success.

# Appendix 1: The Long-Form Improv Glossary

*Blackout*—A blackout is an extremely quick scene, lasting only a few lines, with setups and punch lines. They are often used in Second City revues to break up the rhythm of the performance and provide a quick, big laugh.

*Callback*—A callback is anything within a scene that somehow refers to something earlier in the long-form piece. It could be a recurring character, situation, location, object—anything that ties things together and forms a kind of pattern.

*Cutaway/cut-to/cut-back*—First utilized in the Movie form, "cut-to" is a verbal edit. If someone in a scene is referring to an event of some kind, the outside player will come on stage and say, "We take you to that moment," or "Cut to: that moment." Once the moment is reviewed, the players may go back to the previous scene by announcing "Cut back."

*Deconstruction*—A long form taught at ImprovOlympic that takes a relatively long opening scene that contains a lot of information and then, in a series of scenes following the opening scenes, integrating portions of the opening scene either tangentially or literally in theme and content.

*Edit*—An edit is a conscious decision on the part of a player or players in an improvisational piece to consciously end a scene and begin a new one. A player within the existing scene can choose to edit himself or herself by initiating an end to the scene, either by walking off stage or simply dropping dead. Any player within the ensemble can also edit the scene by making a strong physical or verbal initiation, strong enough that the people in the current scene *know* you are initiating a new scene.

*Game in the scene*—The game is the source of the comedy in scenes from the beginnings of comedy to today. One game may be one-

upmanship, in which two players try to top each other somehow with each remark they say. It is the job of the improviser to
sense the game in the scene and then play it to the best of her
ability, heightening everything her partner gives.

*Group mind*—This is the pinnacle of what an improviser seeks. The
group mind is a long-form improvisational ensemble that is so
closely connected they can anticipate each other's moves.

*Harold*—First created by Del Close at the Committee in the late
1960s and then re-created by Close and Charna Halpern in
Chicago circa 1983, this long form is explained in detail in their
book *Truth in Comedy*. It created a second revolution in improvisational theatre by proving that improvisation without any written material could withstand the scrutiny of a paying audience
for an evening's entertainment.

*La Ronde*—A long-form exercise in which two players, Characters A
and B, sit on stage together. They do a scene and Character C
comes into the scene and tags Character A out. B and C proceed
to do a scene in a new situation. Character D then comes in and
tags out Character B and so on until the final character who enters is Character A, completing the circle.

*Monologue*—A monologue in improv is just like a monologue in
written theatre except it is improvised. Often used to punctuate
scenes; often used in openings. Monologues in long forms need
to be short since the scene's the thing in improv.

*Movie*—Another long form created at ImprovOlympic, the Movie is
more of a narrative long form than the Harold or Deconstruction in that it attempts to re-create an improvised movie on
stage, utilizing onstage "camera" tricks. No longer performed or
taught at ImprovOlympic, the form is still alive with IO alumni
at the Upright Citizens Brigade Theater in New York.

*Object work and environment*—It is the job of the improviser to create objects out of thin air and have enough conviction in the
objects he holds and the environment he creates that the audience believes those objects and that environment are really on
stage with the performers.

*Opening*—The group game or scene or series of monologues that
immediately follows the audience suggestion in a traditional
ImprovOlympic Harold. Teams often have a set opening, like
the Cocktail Party, or may make it up on the spot. It is often

utilized to riff off the suggestion and create multiple starting points for games and scenes.

*Pimping*—One of the big no-no's in improv. A typical pimp would be saying to your partner, "Say, why don't you do that little dance you used to do!" Since it would be un-improv-like to deny your line, your partner is then trapped into doing what you tell her to do. Pimping is never good.

*Rule of threes*—Applicable not only in improv but writing, the rule of threes is a guideline to how many times one can say the same thing. It follows the "beginning, middle, end" idea of narrative writing. The number three is the most dominant number in art.

*Show, don't tell*—A credo that applies in most storytelling. If a player on stage says, "Let's go to Grandma's," the audience wants to see you go to Grandma's, not talk about it. There's more opportunity in moving forward.

*Split scene*—Two scenes occurring in tandem, usually stage left and stage right. They are connected in the long-form piece by sharing a theme or a situation. They are separate scenes taking place in separate locations.

*Start in the middle*—This credo in improv means one should enter a scene with the mindset that she is joining a scene in progress. Needless exposition is then eliminated.

*Sweep edit*—This is the most common kind of edit in a long-form piece, in which a player will simply walk across the stage, downstage of the current scene.

*Stomp edit*—A less refined version of the sweep edit in which the editor literally stomps on stage. Not recommended, especially if your stage is a little rickety.

*Tagout*—Literally, someone enters a scene, tags a person in the scene, and takes her place. It is a more physical version of the verbal cut-to edit. A tagout results in taking focus. The person tagging out then initiates something new, introducing a new character in the context of the previous scene or starting a new scene altogether. Jazz Freddy is credited by many for introducing this technique to long-form improvisation.

*Take focus/give focus*—Giving the focus of the scene to the other player is the job of the long-form improviser. Taking focus is discouraged.

*The "out"*—In a Harold and other long forms, it is often the job of the person in the light booth to take down the lights, ending the long-form piece. He or she needs to find the "out," which is an appropriate point at which to end the piece. It can be a big laugh, it can be the climax of a scene, etc.

*Time Dash*—A game that forms the basis of the ImprovOlympic version of the Harold. A scene is played out and then the players show the events that both precede and follow the events in the scene. They could initiate a scene that takes place fifty years before the scene or perhaps five minutes afterward.

*Top of your intelligence*—Another of the vastly important rules, this means you cannot pretend to be less intelligent than you really are, for example, pretending you don't know something when you *do* know it, like not knowing what a chiropractor is when you really do. On the flip side, pretending you know what something is when you really don't is also a no-no in improv.

*Walk-on*—A walk-on is when a new player joins a scene in progress. To be used sparingly, the walk-on is only appropriate when heightening the existing scene and not when you are stealing focus. Walk-ons generally are quickly followed by the walk-off.

*We see*—A brief walk-on in which a player not in the scene will describe something in the environment and then walk off.

# ppendix 2: Chicago Improv Training

Annoyance Productions
3036 N. Lincoln Avenue, Suite 3A
Chicago, IL 60657
(773) 728-4111
*www.annoyanceproductions.com*

Creators of *Co-Ed Prison Sluts* and *The Real Live Brady Bunch,* Annoyance founder Mick Napier and fellow teachers teach improv classes following their philosophy of free performance. The Annoyance is one of the premiere training centers for improvisers interested in freeing themselves on stage.

---

ImprovOlympic
3541 N. Clark
Chicago, IL 60613
Contact: Liz Allen
(773) 880-9993
*www.improvolympic.com*

The home of the Harold and the Chicago improv revolution of the '80s and '90s.

---

The Playground Improv Theater
3341 N. Lincoln Avenue
Chicago, IL 60657
Contact: Lillie Frances
(773) 871-3793
*www.the-playground.com*

Chicago's improv co-op offers Master's classes, advanced workshops intended for students who have completed programs at Annoyance, ImprovOlympic, or Second City.

---

Players Workshop
777 N. Green Street
Chicago, IL 60622
(312) 377-8757
*www.playersworkshop.com*

Players Workshop is the *oldest school* of improvisation in Chicago. For over thirty-five years, Josephine Forsberg and her staff have trained actors, writers, and other creative professionals to become better at what they do. Players Workshop supplied Second City with much talent before they began their own training center in the mid-'80s. It is recommended for beginners.

---

The Second City Training Center
1616 N. Wells
Chicago, IL 60614
Contact: Rob Chambers
(312) 337-3992
*www.secondcity.com*

The training center for one of Chicago's most treasured institutions, the Second City Training Center has several programs available for those interested in writing and improvisation.

---

WNEP Theater
3210 N. Halsted
Chicago, IL 60657
*www.wneptheater.org*

Masters classes are taught by various instructors covering both improvisation and traditional theatre. Improv classes are focused on the Meisner-based technique, taught by its popularizer, Rob Mello.

Chicago Comedy Company
3807 N. Ashland
Chicago, IL 60613
(773) 528-0032
*www.chicagocomedyco.com*

Chicago Comedy Company, whose specialty in corporate entertainment has made it one of the most successful improv ventures in recent years, began teaching workshops in late 2001, focusing on people in the business world who wish to improve their creativity and confidence. They also teach workshops for improvisers and actors.

# Bibliography

Adler, Tony. 1993. "Company Finds Art in Improv." *Chicago Tribune* 11 May.

Close, Del, Charna Halpern, and Kim "Howard" Johnson. 1994. *Truth in Comedy: The Manual of Improvisation.* Colorado Springs: Meriwether.

Coleman, Janet. 1990. *The Compass: The Improvisational Theatre That Revolutionized American Comedy.* Chicago: University of Chicago Press.

Johnstone, Keith. 1979. *Impro: Improvisation and the Theatre.* New York: Faber and Faber.

Jones, Chris. 1997. "Artswatch." *Chicago Tribune* 12 October.

Kaufman, Carrie L. 2000. "Living in the Moment." *PerformInk* 14 April.

Kogan, Rick. 1985. "Competing for Laughs, 'Harold' Fills House." *Chicago Tribune* 16 August.

———. 1987. "Improv Is Flowing into Mainstream." *Chicago Tribune* 15 February.

———. 1989. "Two Joints That Swing in the Night." *Chicago Tribune* 13 August.

———. 1990. "Playing the Adventurous Improv Tune." *Chicago Tribune* 10 June.

Lavin, Cheryl. 1991. ". . . 3-2-1: Quick! Be Funny! Fear? Ha! Team Keeps Cool Heading for the Super Bowl of Improvisational Comedy." *Chicago Tribune* 24 February.

Moffitt, D. E. n.d. "Viola Spolin Biography." *Spolin Center.* Available at *www.spolin.com/violabio.html.*

Obejas, Achy. 2001. "Comedy Guru Charna Halpern Carries On." *Chicago Tribune* 3 April.

Patinkin, Sheldon. 2000. *The Second City: Backstage at the World's Greatest Comedy Theater.* Naperville, IL: Sourcebooks Trade.

"Sanford Meisner's Bio." *The Sanford Meisner Center.* Available at *www.themeisnercenter.com/meisnerBio.html.*

Spolin, Viola, Paul Sills, and William Sills. 1999. *Improvisation for the Theater.* 3d ed. Evanston, IL: Northwestern University Press.

Sweet, Jeffrey. 1978. *Something Wonderful Right Away.* New York: Avon.

Vogler, Christopher. 1998. *The Writer's Journey: Mythic Structure for Writers.* 2d ed. Studio City, CA: Michael Wiese Productions.

Wolf, Robert. 1986. "When It Comes to Improvisation, There's a New Game in Town." *Chicago Tribune* 23 February.